W9-BDA-612

CHOPIN

FRÉDÉRIC CHOPIN
From a drawing by Franz Liszt

HENRI BIDOU

CHOPIN

TRANSLATED BY

CATHERINE ALISON PHILLIPS

TUDOR PUBLISHING CO.
NEW YORK

Published September, 1927
Second Printing July, 1931
New Edition, May 1936

ORIGINALLY PUBLISHED AS

CHOPIN

MANUFACTURED

IN THE UNITED STATES OF AMERICA

BY MONTAUK BOOKBINDING CORP.

CONTENTS

TRANSLATOR'S NOTE

The translator wishes to acknowledge her indebtedness to Miss Agnes Bedford, editor of Four Mediaeval Songs, *etc., for kindly reading the manuscript and giving her the benefit of her advice.*

LIST OF ILLUSTRATIONS

PART ONE

CHOPIN IN POLAND

1810–1830

CHAPTER 1

FREDERICK FRANCIS CHOPIN was born on February 22, 1810 at six o'clock in the evening at the village of Żelazowa Wola, some twenty versts from Warsaw. "I am a true Mazovian," he wrote later à propos of the powers of illusion characteristic of his race.[1] His birth was registered on April 23rd at Brochów, in the district of Sochaczew, department of Warsaw. The entry was discovered in 1893 by Father Bielawski, parish priest of Brochów.[2]

His father, Nicholas Chopin (Chopyn in the entry of his birth), was born at Nancy on August 17, 1770. Nothing is known of his origin. The Polish historian Szulc [3] records a tradition that Nicholas Chopin was descended from a Polish nobleman who had gone to Lorraine with Stanislas Leszczyński.[4] On arriving in France he was alleged to have taken the name of Chopin. Karasowski, a friend of the family, says nothing of this story. It was mentioned in 1886, in Count

[1] The notes will be found at the end of each part.

Wodziński's book.[5] There is no documentary evidence to confirm it.

Whether he was a Pole or a Lorrainer by origin, Nicholas Chopin was at Warsaw in 1787. He was summoned there by a Frenchman who had a tobacco factory and required a cashier.[6]

Fifteen years previously, Poland had met with a terrible catastrophe. In September, 1772, her three neighbours, Russia, Prussia and Austria, had deprived her, in time of peace, of part of her provinces. The Partition was ratified by a diet which opened at Warsaw on April 19, 1773, under the threat of the Russian bayonets; and Poland was kept in tutelage by a permanent council, under the influence of Muscovite ambassadors. Under the stress of these cruel trials, Poland attempted to reform herself. The diet of 1776 entrusted the preparation of a code to Andrew Zamoyski. The intrigues of the partitioning powers caused this code to be rejected by the diet of 1780. When Nicholas Chopin arrived in Poland, the great diet of 1788 was about to meet. It drew up a constitution which was promulgated on May 3, 1791.

Once again Russia stirred up dissension. On May 14, 1792, the dissidents formed the Confederation of Targowica. The king marched against them; then, by order of Catherine II, concluded the war and disavowed the work of the constituent diet. On April 9, 1793, Russia and Prussia declared their intention of once more partitioning Poland. As had happened twenty years before, this second partition was ratified at Grodno by a diet surrounded by Russian soldiers.

But in the spring of 1794 Poland rose in revolt. On March 24 the inhabitants of Cracow chose as their commander-in-chief Thaddeus Kościuszko. For ten months he kept up the struggle. On October 10 he was wounded and taken prisoner at Macieiowice. On November 5, Praga, the suburb of Warsaw on the opposite side of the Vistula, was captured by Suvorov. What was left of Poland was obliterated from the map by a third partition, and King Stanislas Leszczyński signed his abdication on November 25, 1795.

The tobacco factory had been shut. Nicholas Chopin thought of returning to France, but fell ill. During the insurrection he enrolled himself in the National Guard, in which he became a captain. He was at Praga on November 5; his company was relieved a few hours before the fall of the city, or he would doubtless have perished. Once again he desired to return to France, and once again he was prevented by illness. He earned his living by giving lessons in French. He became tutor to the four children of Starościna Łonszyńska, one of whose daughters was the celebrated Countess Maria Walewska. Then in 1800 he became tutor to the son of the Countess Skarbek, at Żelazowa Wola.[7]

It was there that Nicholas Chopin met Justina Krzyżanowska. She was poor, but of noble birth. He married her on June 2, 1806. He was thirty-seven years of age and his wife twenty-four. They had a daughter Louise, and then a son, who was the musician. Two other daughters were born, Isabelle on July 9, 1811, and Emilienne in 1813.[8]

In a book published in 1886, Count Wodziński has given a poetic description of Żelazowa Wola. "Polish villages are all alike," he says, "a clump of trees surrounding the *dwór,* or nobleman's house; the barns, cow-houses and stables form a spacious square courtyard, in the middle of which a well has been sunk, to which the red-turbaned girls go to fill their pails; roads planted with poplars and fringed with thatched huts; then fields of rye and wheat, stirred by the wind as with rippling waves, gilded and gleaming in the sun; fields of yellow-blossomed colza, lucerne and silvery clover; then forests which, in proportion as they are more or less remote, either stand out in dark masses against the horizon, or stretch out like a girdle of blue, or shimmer in a gauzy vapour. "Such," says Count Wodzinski, "is Żelazowa Wola. A few feet away from the castle, I paused in front of a little slate-roofed house, flanked with a small flight of wooden steps. Nothing has changed for nearly a hundred years. It is crossed by a gloomy vestibule. On the left, in a room lit by the ruddy flame of slowly burning logs, or by the flickering light of two candles placed one at each end of a long table, the serving maids spin as in olden days, relating to each other a thousand wondrous legends." On the right, the residence consists of three rooms, so low that one can touch the ceiling with one's finger. This is the house in which Chopin was born.[9]

In 1807, however, Napoleon restored a shadowy Poland. On October 1, 1810, Nicholas Chopin was appointed professor of French at the Warsaw Lyceum, and the family took up their residence in the city. In 1812 he obtained a similar position at the School of Artillery and Military Engineering, and in 1815 at the preparatory department of the Military School. He was poorly paid, and added to his resources by opening a boarding school. A few of Frederick Chopin's most intimate friends, Titus Woyciechowski, Fontana, and the Wodzinski brothers, were pupils of his father.[10]

It is not hard to believe that from his earliest infancy Frederick was so sensitive to music that it made him burst into uncontrollable tears.[11] He showed such a strong taste for the piano that his parents decided to have him given lessons. When he was six years old, they gave him as his master Adalbert Zywny, a Czech pianist who had come to Poland during the reign of Stanislas Leszczyński.[12] According to the testimony of Liszt, Zywny gave Chopin an " entirely classical " education. He was a good, worthy man, not much of a virtuoso, but a good teacher. We have a letter of his written to his pupil in 1835, after Chopin had become famous. It is ceremonious, in the old style, with a gravely affectionate tone of calm simplicity.[13] He was a fervent admirer of Johann Sebastian Bach, and communicated this admiration to his pupil. As late as the year 1839, on Chopin's return from Majorca, when he was convalescent and working very little, he wrote to his friend Fontana: " I am correcting for my own use a Parisian edition of the works of Bach; not only are there misprints in it, but, I believe, mistakes in harmony, committed by those who set up to understand Bach. I am not doing it with any claim to understand him better than they do, but in the conviction that I can sometimes guess what it ought to be." And how can we deny the affinity between certain of Chopin's most thrilling reveries, and, say, the Andante of the Italian Concerto, with its firmly-knit structure and free melodic line.

On February 24, 1818, at the age of eight, Chopin played a concerto by Adalbert Gyrowetz at a charity concert. The little virtuoso was asked to the houses of the whole of the Polish aristocracy, the Czartoryskis, the Sapiehas, the Czetwertyńskis, the Lubeckis, the Radziwills, the Skarbeks, the Wolickis, the Pruszaks, the Hussarzewskis, the Lempickis. Princess Czetwertyńska presented him to Princess Lowicka, wife of the Grand Duke Constantine. This dread prince took a fancy to the ten-year-old musician, who dedicated a march to him. While the child was playing his piece, the Grand Duke strode up and down the room keeping step to it and beating time. He had the march arranged for orchestra; the military band played it in the Saxon Square, and it was published without the composer's name. Chopin would occasionally improvise. Seeing his eyes raised to the ceiling, the Grand Duke asked him: " Why do you always look upwards, little one? Can you see notes up there? " The Tsar's brother had said a better thing than he supposed.[14] Moreover, as a child Chopin was, as Niecks puts it, "neither an intellectual prodigy nor a conceited puppy, but a naïve, modest child, who played the piano as the birds sing, with unconscious art." [15]

In 1824 his parents sent him to the Lyceum at Warsaw; at the same time requesting Elsner, director of the Conservatoire, to teach him harmony and counterpoint. Elsner was born in Silesia in 1769, studied under Förster at Breslau, became first violin at the theatre at Brunn (Brno) and was settled in Poland by 1792. In spite of his foreign origin, "he became a national composer, or one of the first of them." [16] Conductor at the theatre at Lemberg, and afterwards, in 1799, at the theatre at Warsaw, director of the Conservatoire which was founded in 1821, a prolific rather than original composer of operas, masses, symphonies, cantatas, pieces for the piano or the voice, works on Polish opera and the Polish language, Elsner, though lacking in genius, seems to have been an excellent teacher. He had the merit of not opposing his pupil's original bent. A musician who in 1841 sent some travel notes to the *Neue Zeitschrift für Musik,* calls him the ancestor of modern Polish music, skilful in estimating and prudent in directing original talent: "He does not endeavour, as other professors too often do, to turn out all his pupils from the same mould as that in which he was cast himself. This was not Elsner's way. At a time when everybody in Warsaw thought Chopin was going astray in bad, anti-musical ways, and ought to hold fast to Himmel and Hummel, or else he would do no good, the skilful Elsner had already clearly understood what a germ of poetry there was in this pale young dreamer, he had felt long before that he had before him the founder of a new school of piano music; far from desiring to drive him on a tight rein, he knew that a noble thoroughbred like Chopin must be driven carefully and not thwarted or trained in the ordinary way, if one wants to do any good with him." He allowed him license with regard to the rules and usages of music, saying that extraordinary gifts demanded extraordinary methods. And he was not too scrupulous with regard to the rules himself.

In a report of July 20, 1829, on the examinations at the Conservatoire, Elsner writes: "Lessons in musical composition: Chopin, Frederick, third year student, amazing capabilities, musical genius."

It was during these years of his youth, at the Lyceum and the Conservatoire, that a band of friends formed round Chopin which has come down to posterity along with him. Titus Woyciechowski, Alexander Riembelicski, a highly talented pianist who died prematurely, Wilhelm von Kolberg, John Matuszyński, Stanislas Koźmian, who became president of the Scientific Society at Posen, Hube, Celiński and two charming poets, Eustace Marylski and Dominic Magnuszewski. Julius Fontana, the pianist and composer, must be placed by himself; born in Warsaw in the same year as Chopin, and like him a pupil of Elsner, he emigrated after the catastrophe of 1832 and met Chopin again in Paris.

* * *

At the age of fifteen, Chopin was a lively, gay and fascinating lad. He was full of a spirit of mockery and ridicule which delighted in parody and buffoonery; and he continued to be so until the sufferings due to his malady became intolerable. At Marienbad, in 1836, he was to amuse his friends the Wodzińskis by his "comical pranks" (*polichinades*); Berlioz alluded to his mischievous good humour, "which lent an irresistible attraction to his friends' relations with him." At Nohant he composed pantomimes, in which he improvised at the piano while the young people danced comic ballets. In 1843, George Sand wrote that Mendizabal had dined with her and made Chopin perform all his stock of imitations. He mimicked the Austrian Em-

THE LYCEUM AT WARSAW
From a contemporary print

THE WARSAW CONSERVATORY
From a contemporary print

peror so perfectly that his friends would have trembled for him, says the Princesse de Beauvau, if it had happened in the old days at Vienna.[17] He would impersonate a Polish Jew or a sentimental Englishman. He would parody those who in playing the piano, to use his own expression, "tried to catch pigeons." This jesting spirit is natural to Slavs: "They have a never-failing taste for the joys of mystification, from the wittiest and most farcical to the bitterest and most gloomy, as if they saw in this mocking make-believe an expression of disdain for that superiority which they secretly ascribe to themselves, but which they conceal with the skill and cunning of oppressed people."[18]

The whole Chopin family was clever and literary. They used to act private theatricals, and the actor Piasecki used to maintain that Frederick would have made an excellent actor. In 1824 he and his sister Emilie, aged eleven, wrote a comedy for their father's birthday, entitled *A Mistake; or The Supposed Thief*. This Emilie, who died at the age of fourteen, was a born poet. She and her sister Isabelle translated a book of Salzmann's tales. Both Isabelle and Louise used to compose books for children.

In Chopin humour and gaiety alternated with that

melancholy which is equally characteristic of the race, that vague yearning, the Polish word for which is *zal*. At Szafarnia, at the house of his friend Dominic Dziewanovski, where he spent his holidays, he would sometimes amuse himself with composing a parody of a newspaper; at other times he would day-dream. He would also mix with the peasants, and listen to their popular tunes.[19]

And so he stored up within him that treasury of national poetry which is the material for a whole side of his work. "The characteristic qualities of our poetic sentiment," says the Polish writer Wilczynski, "are quite peculiar, and differentiate us from all other nations . . . Our land . . . breathes calm and tranquillity. Our spirit is imprisoned by no barriers, and roves at will across endless plains; nothing imposes itself upon it irresistibly — neither desolate rocks nor too brilliant a sky, nor too fierce a sun; nature does not inspire it with too powerful emotions, nor does nature entirely absorb it. Thus the spirit turns towards other objects, and enquiries into the mysteries of life. Hence the free spirit of our poetry, hence, too, its constant tendency towards the beautiful and its passionate pursuit of the ideal. The strength of our poetry lies in its simplicity, in the truth of its emotion, and in its aim, which is always a lofty one. Another of its properties is an unprecedentedly vivid imagination." [20]

This definition of Polish poetry might stand as an epigraph at the head of Chopin's works. And so might this other passage on simplicity of style: "Here we have a simple style, a thing as rare as a flawless pearl. . . . It demands a soul both simple and pure, a poetical imagination and delicacy of feeling. Purity of style raises art to the level of a religion."

Side by side with the landscape and the soul of his country, it was the dance-tunes of Poland which determined his idea of music. Not only did he copy the rhythms of the mazurka, the Krakowiak and the polonaise,[21] but the very outline of his melody has the movement of dance music. "These flexible forms, these balanced and corresponding movements awake in us some vague notion of the dance, and it is, in fact, the dance which has inspired them. The deliberate movement and the length of the phrase . . . together with some other artifices of rhythm and harmony, blur the impression of an actual dance, and lend it the character of an idealised and mysterious pantomime." [22]

In Chopin the very structure of the melody calls up the idea of a dance. Dreamer though he is, his melodies are almost always square. The period is made up of two phrases, each consisting of two figures (*incise*), made up of two motives. The second figure repeats the first motive and changes the second. The second phrase repeats the first figure and changes the second; like two dancers changing partners.

Powerfully impregnated though he was with the very essence of his native soil, Chopin was almost indifferent to nature in later days. "I was not made for the country," he writes from Nohant on July 20, 1845; and the sole concession he will make is to add, "Yet I enjoy the fresh air." At heart he cared for nothing but Paris and its salons. M. Elie Poirée, in the charming book which he has devoted to Chopin, has well summed up this characteristic: "In him," he says, "the impressions of nature did not go beyond either the early years of his youth or the frontiers of his native land; it is these memories to which he goes back later, when he goes on writing polonaises or mazurkas. The countryside of Berry, the landscapes of the Balearics, do not seem to have awakened any artistic sensations in him." [23]

* * *

THE year 1825 was the real starting-point of Chopin's musical career. On May 27 and June 10 he took part in two charity concerts given by Javurek, one of the professors at the Conservatoire. He played Moscheles' Allegro in F Minor, and improvised upon a novel instrument, the aeolopantaleon, a combination of the aeolomelodicon and the piano. He introduced the aeolomelodicon to the Emperor Alexander I, who was at Warsaw. And he composed his first works.

First there was the Rondo in C Minor (op. 1), dedicated to Mme. Linde, the wife of the rector of the Lyceum. Schumann relates that a lady of his acquaintance considered this work "very pretty, very refined, almost reminding one of Moscheles (*moschelesque*)."

Let us pause for a moment over this first work. A rondo is the final movement of a sonata. Its construction is that of the Allegro, except that the opening subject, forming the theme, is repeated as a refrain at the end of the first section. At the age of fifteen Chopin did not yet venture to compose a whole sonata. But, like a good Conservatoire student, he goes straight to this, the highest form of composition, and we shall see him applying the rules taught him by Elsner. He applies them for two pages, and then he allows himself to be carried away at his own sweet will, and these youthful and sometimes errant caprices, together with a natural grace and gaily varied colour, make up the charm of this essay.

The piece begins with a sort of introduction of four bars establishing the key of C by striking alternately the tonic and the dominant.

Next comes a first period [24] of eight bars, the melodic formula of which is as follows:

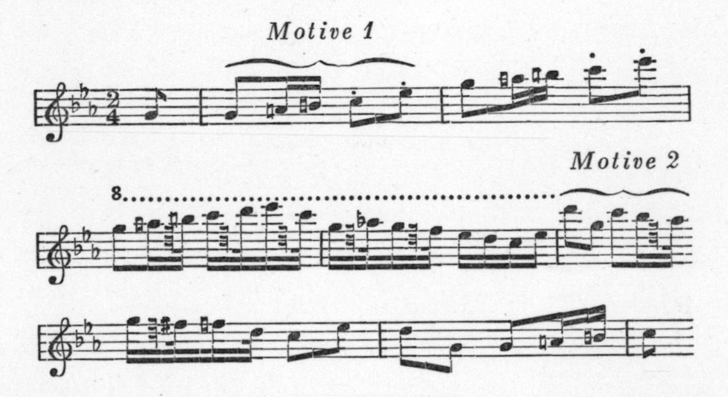

We see at once that this period falls into two phrases, each of which contains a motive. These two motives, like the introduction, are based on the dominant and the tonic. They form only one, for the second is nothing but the first inverted.

A second period repeats the first phrase in the relative major and the second phrase unchanged. A third flutters its wings and goes off in a running passage to come to rest in turn on the unchanged second phrase. This flight is the first attempt at the long phrase, broadly projected yet delicately outlined, which is characteristic of Chopin. These three periods form the first group, what composers call the *groupe de thème* (exposition section or first subject). Then begins what French composers call a *divertissement* and German composers a *groupe de transition* (bridge-passage). This also begins with a period of eight bars, of which the melodic plan is as follows:

This period is merely a phrase repeated; and this phrase is made up of two figures, themselves constructed upon two motives. The first motive is a variant of the introduction; the second motive is a fresh one. A second period is linked on to this motive, and transforms it. The composer is in a sportive mood. Another *divertissement* ensues, repeated in A minor and E minor. Here a scale acts as a transition leading us to

E major, and introduces a third group, known as the *groupe de chant* (second subject).

This phrase, played with slackened tempo, and of which the somewhat commonplace weakness is only too noticeable, is repeated to form the period, which is itself repeated with no change. This theme is not developed, strictly speaking, but its rhythm, kept up as it were by the hand, gives rise to another phrase. This latter phrase passes from E major to the relative C sharp minor, then to D sharp minor, and finally to G sharp minor. Having arrived at this key, Chopin, carried away by the music, allows himself to float in a cloud of sparkling arpeggi, in which it is hard to recognise any melodic theme. Weary of this, he makes an enharmonic change to the key of A flat, and then begins one of those harmonic progressions of which he was to become so fond, and in which his contemporaries were to see as it were his signature. Here is the first period of it.

This progression leads up to the chord of G, upon which Chopin constructs a period of eleven bars, practically amounting to a cadence, for this insistent G is merely the dominant of the key of C minor, to which the composer wants to bring us back in order to repeat in it the two first groups, characterising the rondo. When this repeat is over, we pass into D flat major, and arrive at the most important section in the whole piece, what is called the *groupe du travail thématique* (development section). In it the composer, having already stated all his themes, brings them together, combines them and develops them, thereby exhibiting his virtuosity. It must be admitted that here the fifteen-year-old virtuoso has fallen back a little upon pianistic rather than musical devices. After a strongly rhythmical episode, in which there is a scale passage for the left hand, just as in the first theme there was one for the right hand, he goes up and down the keyboard with answering arpeggi and contrasted figures. He next repeats, according to the classical formula, but this time it is the second subject and the cadential group, transposing each a second into D flat minor, which is perhaps a reminiscence of his exercises in fugue. Finally the chord of G once more brings him back into the key of C minor, and he ends up with the theme.

The work is undoubtedly of no very great originality; Niecks will not admit any imitation in it of another master; yet it is difficult not to think of Hummel's rondos. But if it is not a profound work, it is not a childish one either. It has two defects from which Chopin never freed himself in his larger compositions: a certain lack of coherence between the parts and a certain emptiness in the development. But an easy, calm breadth, richly coloured harmony, and elegance of writing are already to be found in it. His powers of melodic invention, which were later to be so abundant and so beautiful, are still dormant in this peaceful child-like heart. The work was published by Brzezina at Warsaw, and gave Chopin for the first time the pleasure of seeing himself in print.

In this same year, 1825, the lad also composed a polonaise in G sharp minor, two mazurkas, one in G, the other in B flat, and some variations on a German air.

Like most of the works of his early youth, these were not published in his life-time. They appeared among the posthumous works. There is no occasion to linger over works which Chopin left lying in his portfolios. Let us, however, say a word about the Polonaise.

Liszt, who had gleaned the tradition in Poland, has given the following brilliant description of the Polonaise: "It was by this dance that the master of the house opened every ball, not with the youngest or most beautiful, but with the most honoured — often the oldest — of the ladies present. . . . After the master of the house followed the most important men, choosing . . . some their favourite ladies, some the most influential among them. The host . . . was bound to lead the train which followed him in order as its leader, in a thousand capricious windings, through all the apartments, in which thronged the rest of the guests. . . ." [25]

When the master of the house had opened the dance, a guest took his place; he himself then took the hand of the second lady, whose partner took the hand of the third, and so on, so that each man stepped a place back, the ladies remaining where they were. The new leader made it a point of honour to outdo his predecessor in leading the train through windings, arabesques and figures. Sometimes he would offer his lady one hand after the other, passing to right or left of her, and all the men imitated him. "It was no commonplace, meaningless procession which they thus performed; it was a parade, or, if we may use the expression, society as a whole showing off its plumage and taking a delight in seeing itself so fine, so noble, so stately and so polished."

We have no polonaise music dating back further than the middle of the eighteenth century. The earliest surviving tunes are grave and sweet. Some of them are like chants of mourning. Count Ogiński [26] infused into his a tender melancholy. In those of Lipiński [27] "the melody becomes more and more clearly defined, diffusing a fragrance of spring-like youth and love. . . . Mayseder continued this tendency trammelled by no national bonds; [28] he ended by attaining a most sprightly coquetry and a charmingly spirited concert-room effect. His imitators have flooded us with pieces called polonaises, whose character no longer justifies their name." [29]

When Weber, who was a great traveller, wrote his Polonaise in E flat (op. 21), had he an intuitive insight into ancient Poland? At one stroke he restored the style. He made it "a dithyramb, in which all the vanished splendours suddenly reappeared. . . . He accentuated the rhythm, used melody as a means of narration, and lent it, by modulation, a profusion of colour which the subject not only admitted, but urgently demanded. He infused life, warmth and passion into the polonaise, without departing from that pride of bearing, that ceremonious and lordly dignity, and that majesty, both natural and conventional, which are inherent in it." Chopin owed a great deal to Weber, and was certainly inspired by the Polonaise in E flat. But, on the one hand, he introduced into it a richer harmony and a more moving touch; and, on the other, he did not by any means always abstain from changing its original uniform character. Even in this stately form of music, he often reverted to that intimate quality which he loved. So Liszt implies by an ingenious figure of speech: "More than once, as he gazed upon the groupings of the brilliant crowd flowing past him, he became enamoured of some isolated figure . . . and sang for her alone."

From the point of view of form, the polonaise is a dance in three-four time, or rather a march admitting of an element of pantomime, in the leader at any rate. It is characterised by a vigorous attack on the strong beat of the bar, and the rhythm

It ends on the third beat:

or on the second and third:

Chopin begins his Polonaise in G sharp minor as he began his Rondo, that is to say, by striking the tonic and the dominant alternately, the common chord of the tonic and the chord of the dominant seventh, in fact. Only he applies to them the strict polonaise rhythm, giving the following figure.

But save for the frequent repetition of this rhythm, the piece is constructed very much on the usual lines of the *lied*, i.e. in three sections. The principal section consists of two groups. The first group is merely a period of two phrases; the motive of the first, reduced to its simplest form, would run as follows:

And the motive of the second thus:

Only Chopin begins these motives with embroideries and appoggiaturas which lend them considerable grace. After a short phrase which reintroduces the principal motive, the second group repeats the first with different and very luxuriant embroideries. Next comes a trio in the relative major; it is likewise made up of two groups, and followed by a repetition of the first group which ends the piece. The whole is very florid, enriched with a wealth of spread chords which hardly conceal the extreme simplicity of the structure, recalling the technique of Weber's brilliant pieces.

CHAPTER 2

In 1826, during the holidays, Madame Chopin took her daughter Emilie, whose chest was weak, to the waters of Reinerz in Silesia. Louise and Frederick accompanied them.[1] From Reinerz the young man went to Strzyżewo to stay with his godmother, Mme. Wiesolowska, a sister of Count Skarbek. Prince Radziwill, governor of the Grand Duchy of Posen, invited him to Antonin, his country place close by. The prince, who was connected with the Prussian royal family through his wife, was a very great person. He was also an enthusiastic musician. He had a fine tenor voice. Every week he played the violoncello in quartets held at his house. And lastly, he composed. He wrote a setting for the first part of *Faust,* which was performed annually at the Berlin Singakademie, the performances continuing till as late as 1879. Young Chopin gradually became a regular guest at Antonin. He made music with the prince and the young princesses. It was here that he wrote several pieces, with a part for solo 'cello.

To the year 1826 is attributed the Polonaise in B minor, entitled *Adieu* and dedicated to Wilhelm von Kolberg. This work was not published till after the composer's death. Chopin's style appears in it more clearly than in the first Rondo. A graceful, tender sensibility, an enchanting delicacy of composition, a highly characteristic flexibility of the melodic line, a charming taste in the ornaments with which the themes are embroidered, already reveal the musician's characteristic qualities. The trio, in D flat minor, is composed on a theme from *La Gazza Ladra,* delicately elaborated. And perhaps this gives us some idea of what Chopin used to play on the piano when he was asked to improvise on a theme.

In 1827 Chopin finished his studies at the *Lyceum,* and was free to pass a few weeks at Strzyźewo; then he went to Danzig, to the house of Superintendent Linde, the rector's brother. It was in this year, 1827, that he wrote the second composition printed at Warsaw, and republished a few years later in Germany, the Rondo in the Style of a Mazurka, in F major (op. 5), dedicated to Countess Alexandrine de Moriolles. He also finished the Polonaise in D minor and the Nocturne in E minor, which were only published among his posthumous works. When Schumann, in 1836, described the Rondo in the Style of a Mazurka, the only traces of the composer's extreme youth which he saw in it were a few rather involved passages from which he did not know how to extricate himself quickly enough; for the rest, the Rondo is quite in Chopin's style, full of beauty, ardour, and grace.[2] "Chopin's personality and nationality," writes Niecks, "begin to be plain beyond a doubt. Who could fail to recognise him in the peculiar sweet and persuasive flows of sound, and the serpent-like winding of the melodic outline, the wide-spread chords, the chromatic progressions, the dissolving of the harmonies, and the linking of their constituent parts?"

Let us examine the structure of the piece. The theme group is formed entirely by the following figure:

repeated, with a modulation into the relative minor, for thirty-six bars. With the transition group, Chopin returns to his system of the period with two motives, each motive being repeated four times in loose sequence to form a phrase. The first motive is as follows:

The second as follows:

The first two periods in the group are merely a repetition of each other; but in the following ones, the rhythm of the second motive passes into the left hand, while the right hand has an ornamental passage in triplets. A harmonic progression brings us to the dominant of the key of B flat minor, which is that of the second subject. Here, for the first time, no doubt, in Chopin's works, we find an admirable melody, of rather an Italian character, extending over a whole period, and accompanied by a strongly marked mazurka rhythm on a tonic pedal:

He sets out this period for a second time, a very expressive sort of bridge passage in C minor forms the third period, while the fourth is a repetition of the first, with the addition of nothing but a great closing arpeggio, which is repeated through a series of modulations, and trails forlornly down the keyboard like a drooping garland four times in succession. This whole group of four periods, constituting the second subject, forms in itself a section of great beauty in Chopin's characteristic style.

*   *   *

We have now arrived at the year 1828. Freed from school, the lad can now give all his time to music.[3] His works now begin to accumulate. Our information is contained in a letter of November 9, 1828, to Titus Woyciechowski:

" At Strzyżewo " (where he passed all the summer) " I rearranged the Rondo in C minor (which you may remember) for two pianos. Today I tried it over with Ernemann at Buchholtz's rooms.[4] We are planning to play it one day at La Ressource. As for my new compositions, I have nothing to show but the still unfinished trio (in G minor), which I started after you went away. I have already tried over the first Allegro, with the accompaniment. I think this trio will have the same fate as my sonata and the variations. These two works are now in Vienna (in the hands of the publisher Haslinger): I have dedicated the former to Elsner, as his pupil; on the second I have, perhaps too boldly, inscribed your name." [5]

Thus the works finished in 1828 were: (1) the Rondo

in C major for two pianos; (2) a Polonaise in B flat major which Chopin does not mention;[6] (3) the Sonata in C minor (op. 4), dedicated to Elsner; (4) the Variations on *La ci darem la mano* (op. 2), dedicated to Titus Woyciechowski.

These Variations became a leading piece in his concert programmes. Haslinger published them in Vienna at the beginning of 1830, and Schumann described them in 1831 in a delightful article in the *Allgemeine Musikalische Zeitung*.

" Eusebius came in softly the other day. You know that ironic smile on his pale face with which he tries to mystify one. I was at the piano with Florestan. . . . Eusebius placed a piece of music before us with these words: ' Hats off to genius, gentlemen! ' We were not allowed to see the title.

" I turned over the pages mechanically: the mysterious joy of music without sound has something enchanting about it. Besides, it appears to me that every composer's manuscript presents to our eyes a peculiar physiognomy of its own: Beethoven has a different look from Mozart on paper. . . . But now I imagined that eyes quite unknown, the eyes of flowers, of basilisks, of peacocks, the eyes of young girls, were gazing at me in wondering wise. In many places it began to seem plainer: I thought I perceived Mozart's *La ci darem la mano* entwined with a hundred chords: Leporello seemed actually to wink at me, and Don Giovanni flitted before me in a white cloak.

"'Play it!' said Florestan. Eusebius consented, and we listened, ensconced in a window seat. Eusebius played as though inspired, making a procession of innumerable figures, animated with the most vivid life, pass before us. But what was the astonishment of his audience on reading beneath the title: opus 2? Through the exclamations we could hear people saying, 'Yes, at last we have come to something perfect. . . . Chopin . . . I have never heard that name. . . . Who can that be? . . . In any case . . . a genius!'" [7]

Here, for the first time, we grasp the dramatic character of Chopin's compositions, as well-defined as the oratorical style of Beethoven's works. And once again it is Schumann who has brought out the point. "The first variation," he says, "might be considered a little too full of distinction and coquetry: the grandee of Spain flirting charmingly with a peasant girl. This rights itself of its own accord in the second, which is already much more intimate, more comic and more teasing, like two lovers pursuing each other, laughing at their own play. What a difference in the third!

Moonlight in February; Mazetto standing aside, and swearing, quite distinctly; but Don Giovanni is not stopped by such a trifle." Next Schumann proceeds to the fourth variation, so daring and challenging, then to the Adagio, in B flat minor, which is like a warning: "Leporello, hiding behind a bush, defies his master; the clarinet and oboe charm us with wooing strains; suddenly the key of D flat major is introduced to indicate the first kiss. . . . But all this is nothing to the finale. Corks pop, bottles are smashed. Then follow the voice of Leporello, the apparition of the spirits, the flight of Don Giovanni, and lastly, a few closing bars of calm and farewell."

We have seen that during this same summer of 1828, Chopin was working at the Trio in G minor for piano, violin and 'cello, which he finished in 1829. Much later, in 1840, when he was working at this trio with Mme. Streicher, Chopin said to her: "I shall always remember the time when I composed it. It was in Posen, at Prince Radziwill's country house in the midst of the forests. A small but chosen company was gathered there. In the morning there was hunting, in the evening music. And now," he added sadly, "the prince, his wife, his son, all, all are dead."

THE letter of September 9 announced to Woyciechowski another piece of news at which Chopin was in transports of joy: he was starting that very day for Berlin. His parents had decided that he was to see Vienna or Berlin on the first favourable occasion. Dr. Jarocki, a professor at the University of Warsaw, had been invited by the University of Berlin to a congress of naturalists presided over by Humboldt, and proposed to take Frederick with him. Circumstances were particularly favourable, as Chopin explains, in that Jarocki was the pupil and friend of Lichtenstein, who was secretary to the congress, but also a member of the Singakademie. Through Lichtenstein, he counted upon making the acquaintance of all the musicians in Berlin, with the exception of Spontini. But Spontini could be got at through Prince Radziwill.

Starting on the 9th, the travellers arrived at Berlin five days later — on the 14th, that is to say — about three in the afternoon. They stopped at the Kronprinz Hotel. That very day Chopin saw Lichtenstein. On Tuesday, the 16th, he wrote his parents one of those long, affectionate, spontaneous letters of his, all alive with his recent impressions, which are so charming. He regretted not having seen Schlesinger, whose library interested him more than any other collection.[8] He had visited Kisting's piano-factory, but there had been no finished instruments there. On the 20th there was another letter. " As if it were done specially for me, the theatre gives a different work every day. First I heard an oratorio at the Singakademie, and at the Opera *Ferdinand Cortez*,[9] *Il matrimonio segreto* and Onslow's *Colporteur*. I followed these operas with great pleasure. But I must admit that Händel's *Ode on St. Cecilia's Day* gripped me; it was what came nearest to that ideal of sublime music which I bear in the depths of my soul." He adds that the performance admitted of a few " buts," but that perhaps it was only in Paris that these " buts " would disappear. On the following day they were to give *Der Freischütz*. " This is the fulfilment of one of my dearest wishes," writes Chopin; " when I have heard it, I shall be able to compare our singers with those here." [10]

After a stay of a fortnight, Chopin and Jarocki started on their way home. There are pleasing anecdotes of the lad playing on whatever piano he found at the inns where they changed horses — they were sometimes good ones — and charming the postmasters. On October 6 he was at Warsaw.

In 1829 Hummel came to Warsaw. In the previous

year he had published his *Piano School* (*Anweisung zum Pianofortespiel*). Chopin and he were sympathetic to each other, but we do not know what impressions the sensitive young Pole received of the cold, brilliant virtuoso. Nor do we know what he thought of Paganini, who also came to Warsaw that year. At any rate, he always spoke of him with admiration.

During this time he composed the Grand Fantasia on Polish Airs for piano and orchestra, the Krakowiak,[11] a Polonaise in F minor, three Waltzes (B minor, D flat major and E major), a Funeral March in C minor. The Polonaises, the Waltzes and the Funeral March appear among the posthumous works. The Fantasia and the Krakowiak were published in 1834 as op. 13 and 14. The compositions of this period are still pieces of virtuosity, intended to display the pianist's powers by transcendent difficulties of execution. And this pianist was one who belonged to the Viennese school, which was trying, during the decline of the classical period, to arrive at a style of playing characterised by lightness and rapidity. But the force of the thought and emotion are already remarkable. The national character, made up of fire, nobility and grace, but also of eccentricity and wildness, struck Schumann, who congratulated Chopin a little later, at the period of the concertos, upon gradually ridding himself of this "Sarmatian" stamp. Moreover, this art, national and personal as it was, was nurtured on the best masters, Beethoven, Schubert and Field: "The first of them formed his spirit for audacity, the second his heart for tenderness, and the third his hand for cunning." [12]

CHAPTER 3

In 1829 Chopin was nineteen years old. He was famous at Warsaw. But this local praise was no longer enough for him. What would be the judgment of a town like Vienna, which had heard Haydn, Mozart and Beethoven?

In the middle of July, 1829, he left for Vienna with his friends Celiński, Hube and Franz Maciejowski. They passed through Cracow, where they spent a week, and by way of Silesia and Moravia arrived in Vienna on July 31.

Elsner had given him a letter to Haslinger, the publisher, who was keeping several of his compositions, but had not published any so far. The Sonata in C minor, which is numbered op. 4, had been left with him in 1828. Haslinger gave a hearty welcome to the young musician. He was so friendly that he hardly knew which chair to offer him: he made his son play to him, and apologised for his wife's being out. He showed him all the new things he was publishing: and announced to him then and there that the Variations on *La ci darem la mano* would appear the following week in the *Odeon*. In order to stimulate the sales he pressed Chopin to give a concert. Chopin had met some of his fellow-countrymen, such as Count Hussarzewski, in whose house he had seen the best society. " It is generally said that the nobility here are extraordinarily pleased with me," he wrote on August 13. And he mentioned the Schwarzenbergs, the Wrbnas, and Count Diedrichstein — the one whom Francis II sent to attend on " L'Aiglon." At Vienna Chopin met Wurfel again, whom he had known as a pianist at Warsaw. Wurfel introduced him to Count Gallenberg, director of the Opera. Gallenberg was all the more inclined to give the young Pole a chance to be heard because he would play for nothing. Chopin hesitated out of shyness. Wurfel implored him not to shame his parents, Elsner and himself by refusing. The journalist Blahetka, whom he had met at Haslinger's, declared that he would make a sensation, and placed him on a par with Moschcles, Herz and Kalkbrenner. Wurfel also introduced him to the amazing Gyrowetz, conductor to the Court and Opera, composer, jurist and diplomatist, who spoke six languages, and left thirty operas, forty ballets, nineteen masses and sixty symphonies, not to mention a formidable mass of chamber-music. Chopin often played works for two pianos with Czerny, who was even more prolific, since he left a thousand or more works. Above all, he was an unrivalled piano teacher, at any rate for the development of speed. "He is a good fellow," writes Chopin, "but nothing more." Yet when it came to saying goodbye, Czerny showed more warmth than did his compositions.

Chopin also made the acquaintance of the famous Schuppanzigh, who was to die a few months later — the first man to interpret Beethoven's quartets. He met the violinist Mayseder, who formed part of the same quartet. He met the composer Konradin Kreutzer, with his pleasing talent, who had been settled in Vienna since 1822, the composer Franz Lachner, then only twenty-six years of age, the composer Seyfried, who wrote for the *Allgemeine Musikalische Zeitung*, and whose brother was also a journalist.[1]

The concert took place on August 11, 1829, at the Imperial Theatre. After Beethoven's *Prometheus* Overture, after some songs by Rossini and Vaccai, sung by Mlle. Veltheim, Chopin was to perform the Variations on *La ci darem la mano* and the Krakowiak for piano and orchestra. But the orchestra had received Chopin with sour looks at the rehearsals, and made so many mistakes, that, by the advice of the manager, the composer had to replace the Krakowiak by two improvisations, one on a theme from *La dame blanche*, the other on the tune of the Polish song *Chmiel.*[2] He sat down to the piano white with rage. Perhaps his rage was an advantage. " I was in despair," he writes to Titus Woyciechowski, " and yet the Variations made such an impression that I was recalled several times. . . . All I know about my improvisation is that it was followed by a thunder of applause and several recalls." [3] The success of the concert induced the organisers to give a second one on the 18th, again without paying Chopin anything. This time, in addition to the Variations, he played the Krakowiak.

The press reflects the charming impression made by the young artist. " The exquisite delicacy of his touch," wrote the *Allgemeine Musikalische Zeitung* for November 18, 1829, " the indescribable dexterity of his technique, the subtle finish of his gradations of tone, reflecting a profoundly sensitive nature, the clearness of his interpretation and of his compositions, which bear the mark of great genius . . . reveal a virtuoso richly endowed by nature, who is appearing on the horizon with no previous advertisement, as one of its most brilliant meteors." What pleased people was the deep sentiment inspiring his art and execution. " His playing and his compositions," says the *Wiener The-*

aterzeitung of August 20, "have a certain modest character, which seems to indicate that this young man's object is not to dazzle, although his execution surmounts all difficulties. . . . His touch is neat, but has not the brilliance displayed by our virtuosi from the very first bars. . . . He plays very quietly, with none of that dash and daring that generally distinguish the artist from the amateur." He is already taken to task for the comparative lack of volume of his tone.[4] Imagining that this weakness was due to the instrument — an excellent piano by Graff — Count Maurice Lichnowsky, the friend of Beethoven, offered him his own piano for the second concert.

After touching farewells and promises of another meeting, Chopin left by coach for Prague, where he arrived on August 21. He took with him letters of introduction from Blahetka and Wurfel, one for the violinist Pixis, conductor at the theatre and a professor at the Conservatoire. At his house he met August Klengel, organist to the court of Dresden, who played to him for two hours his as yet unpublished *Canons and Fugues in all the major and minor keys*,[5] but did not ask him to play.

From Prague Chopin went on to Dresden. He stopped on the way there at Teplitz, and a fellow-countryman,

Louis Lempicki, took him to see Prince Clary. The prince was one of the greatest nobles of Austria. The princess, who had been a Countess Chotek, was an excellent pianist. Chopin describes this visit in a charming letter:

"We went in: it was a small but distinguished party: an Austrian prince, a general, whose name I have forgotten, an English naval captain, a few young men of fashion (I believe they were Austrian princes too), and the Saxon General von Leiser, with an extraordinary number of decorations and a scar on his face. After tea, before which I had talked a great deal to the prince himself, his mother asked me to be so good as to sit down at the piano (a good piano by Graff). I was so good as to do so, but for my part I asked them to be so good as to give me a theme to improvise upon. I at once heard the ladies, who were sitting round a a table, murmuring to one another, 'A theme, a theme. . . .'

"The three pretty young princesses put their heads together, till one of them turned to M. Fritsche, young Clary's tutor. He suggested to me a theme from Rossini's *Moses,* which met with general consent. I improvised, and apparently it was a success." [6]

Chopin left Teplitz on August 26 and arrived that evening in Dresden. Klengel had given him a note for Morlacchi, the conductor of the Italian opera; Morlacchi took him to the house of Mme. Pesadori, a pupil of Klengel and the best pianist in Dresden. Thus he had fresh relays of introductions from one town to another. He returned to Warsaw on September 12, 1829.

CHAPTER 4

CHOPIN was now at home again. The praise of the Viennese critics had given him a taste for travel, and he was very anxious not to spend the winter in his own country. He had, however, begun so many works that the wise course would no doubt have been to finish them in Warsaw. And perhaps he was kept there by another motive. His piano had become the confidant of his heart. " How horrible it is," he writes on October 31, 1829, to Titus Woyciechowski, " when one's heart is oppressed, not to be able to pour forth one's feelings into another heart. You know what I mean. How often do I confide to my piano what I should like to confide to you! "

He was in love with a student at the Conservatoire, Constantia Gladkowska. He had flirted at Vienna with Mlle. Blahetka, who was as pretty as she was clever, and was not yet twenty. On his departure he had given her one of his compositions with a dedication. But in this letter of October 3, in which he mentions to Titus what reasons he had for returning to Vienna, he adds: " You will perhaps think that I am referring to Mlle. Blahetka, about whom I told you; but do not believe it. I have found, perhaps to my misfortune, my ideal, whom I venerate faithfully and truly. It has already lasted for six months, and I have not yet spoken a syllable to her of whom I dream every night. It was with thoughts of this beautiful creature that I composed the Adagio of my new concerto, as well as the valse which I wrote this morning and am sending you. Note the passage marked with a cross. Nobody but you knows what it means. How happy I should be if I could play you my new compositions, my dear friend! In the fifth bar of the trio the deep melody predominates up to the high E flat in the key of G. I ought not to tell you so, for you would have noticed it yourself." [1]

This waltz, composed on the morning of October 3, is the Waltz in D flat major, which appears among the posthumous works (op. 71, no. 2). [2] The trio is in G flat. At the fifth bar the melody, which was previously in the bass, does indeed pass to the right hand. Here is this first well-authenticated lament of his young love:

As for the concerto to which he alludes, this is the Concerto in F minor, which was not published till 1836, as op. 21, dedicated to Countess Potocka. Chopin alludes to it in several letters to Titus. On October 20 he relates how Elsner praised the Adagio, and found a certain novelty in it, but that he, the author, is not yet pleased with the finale. On November 14, in describing his visit to Prince Radziwill at Antonin, where he spent a week, he adds: "I would gladly have prolonged my visit until they turned me out. But my affairs, and above all my concerto, which is still impatiently awaiting its finale, forced me to take leave of this paradise."

The motive of this visit to Antonin was a serious interview with Prince Radziwill, who wished to have Chopin in his household at Berlin. The young man was dubious. "One should not eat cherries with great noblemen," he would say. His father was more credulous, and refused to believe that these promises were nothing but fair words. But as a matter of fact, nothing came of them.

During his week's stay at Antonin, as the guest of a princely musician, Chopin read the Prince's *Faust*, flirted with the two young princesses, and made music. He played Princess Elise the Polonaise in F minor, composed that same year,[3] and she was enthusiastic about it. He wrote another polonaise for piano and 'cello. This was op. 3 in C major (Introduction and Polonaise brillante), published in 1833. He mentions it in the same letter: " I wrote while staying with him an Alla polacca for 'cello. It is a brilliant drawing-room piece for ladies. I should be glad if the Princess Wanda would study it."

By the end of the winter of 1830, the Concerto in F minor was finished, and on March 17 Chopin gave his first concert at Warsaw. The programme was divided into two parts. The first began with the overture from an opera by Elsner.[4] Having paid this tribute to his master, Chopin played his Concerto, which was interrupted after the Allegro by a *divertissement* for the horn composed and played by Gorner. The second part, after an overture from one of Kurpiński's operas and some Variations by Paer, sung by Mme. Meier, ended up with a potpourri of Polish airs.

The Concerto in F minor is now entitled the Second Concerto (op. 21), owing to the late date at which it was published (1836). In Chopin's day the concerto was a sonata in which the statement of the themes is allotted to the orchestra, the development being entrusted to the solo instrument, unfortunately with the object of showing off the brilliancy of the virtuoso. The Concerto in F minor consists of three movements, a Maestoso, a

Larghetto and an Allegro vivace. The Maestoso begins with a long orchestral exposition, which sets forth all the themes one after the other. In accordance with the system then almost uniform in Chopin's work, every period is made up of two phrases of four bars each; every phase consists of a figure repeated, and every figure of two motives. The following is the plan of the first period:

Next comes another period similarly constructed, but with different motives, then a third, then a fourth in the relative major; it is repeated with a few variants and followed by a short development, which prepares for the entry of the solo instrument in the original key. But just as we think that this solo is about to begin, the composer, by a characteristic Chopinesque caprice, holds it back for another eight bars, for a poetic episode, a parenthesis, a dialogue between flute and violin. The pianist then takes up these motives, which the orchestra has given out one after the other; he develops them and mingles them in no clearly-defined order, interspersing them with all kinds of ornaments and brilliant passages.

Niecks has given a charming description of this piece. When, after the themes have been given out by the orchestra, "the piano interrupts the orchestra impatiently, and then takes up the first subject, it is as if we were transported into another world and breathed a purer atmosphere. First there are some questions and expostulations, then the composer unfolds a tale full of sweet melancholy in a strain of lovely, tenderly-entwined melody. With what inimitable grace he winds those delicate garlands around the members of his melodic structure! How light and airy the harmonic base on which it rests! But the contemplation of his grief disturbs his equanimity more and more, and he begins to fret and fume. In the second subject he seems to protest the truthfulness and devotion of his heart, and concludes with a passage, half upbraiding, half beseeching, which is quite captivating, nay more, even bewitching in its eloquent persuasiveness. Thus far, from the entrance of the piano, all was irreproachable."[5]

The Larghetto in A flat major which forms the second movement was composed while he was thinking of Constantia. "While my thoughts were with her," wrote Chopin on October 3, 1829, "I composed the Adagio of my concerto." Love unfortunately inspired him with an operatic phrase which he has adorned with a profusion of false tresses. Let us, however, remember that Schumann and Liszt spoke of it with great admiration, and moreover that it was one of the pieces which Chopin was fondest of playing. The work ends with a light and charming Allegro in F minor.

A few days later there was a second concert. Once again the concerto was the most important feature of the first part,[6] but in the second Chopin gave two pieces: first the Krakowiak for piano and orchestra, in F Major, which he had already played at Vienna, and which was published in 1834 as op. 14; and next, after an aria sung by Mme. Meier,[7] an improvisation on the air: *The Ways of the Town.* The success of the two concerts seems to have been more brilliant than the profits: the net amount was not more than 5,000 gulden, or about £120, although the theatre was full. The Concerto and the Krakowiak were much admired. The official Gazette declared that the Poles would one day be as proud of the young artist as the Germans are of Mozart.

* * *

DURING the summer of 1830, Chopin completed a new concerto in E minor, which was published in 1833 as op. 11. The Allegro and Adagio were written by the middle of May, but the " enthusiastic mood " which he required in order to write the Rondo had not yet come to him. He found it a little later, for on August 21 he writes to Titus that the Rondo is finished.

Constantia Gładkowska made her début in Paer's *Agnes.* Chopin still loved her unhappily. He would have liked to go to Vienna in September, and thence to Milan, but he felt himself to be held at Warsaw. A presentiment of death already mingled with the tortures of young love, and was perhaps no more than one of its forms. Chopin was disheartened, incapable of working or making up his mind. At midday on September 4, not yet dressed or knowing what day it was, he wrote a really desperate letter: "I tell you, I have ideas which grow madder and madder. I am still here and I cannot decide to fix the date of my departure. I still have a presentiment that I am leaving Warsaw never to return. I bear within me the conviction that I am saying farewell to my country for ever. Ah! How sad it must be to die anywhere but in one's birthplace. How hard it would be to see round my deathbed, not the dear faces of my own people, but an indifferent doctor and a paid servant. Believe me, my dear Titus, I should often like to be near you, in order to find rest for my tortured heart. Since that is not possible, I go hurrying along the streets, without knowing why. My ardour is neither appeased nor diverted, and I return home to plunge once more into a nameless desire."

Read this letter over again, thinking it in terms of music. It is made up of linked and recurrent motives: the motive of distraction, the motive of solitude and death, the motive of friendship, the motive of the woman he loved. Then follow sadness, tenderness and reverie. It is a piece by Chopin ready-made.

In order to hoodwink his father, he pretended to be in love with Mlle. de Moriolles. He even went back on his word in writing to Titus on the 18th, as follows: " You are mistaken in thinking, like so many others, that my heart is concerned in the prolongation of my stay here. I assure you that I shall be able to rise superior to my heart when it is a question of my future, and that if I loved, I should succeed in dominating my melancholy and sterile ardour."

But he was as changeable as a true Slav, and on the 4th he declared that he had not yet tried over his concerto, being entirely taken up with his love; his visit to Vienna was to be nothing but an endless series of sighs. On the 18th he is thinking of nothing but work. On the 22nd he writes that his departure has been decided upon; but he is wretched and tormented. Two days before, at church, he had been wounded by a glance from his ideal, as he calls Constantia. "I at once rushed into the street, and it was almost a quarter of an hour before I regained my senses; I am sometimes so mad that I am afraid of myself."

On the same day, however, he gave a rehearsal with orchestra, before the best musical society of Warsaw, of the Concerto in E minor which he had just finished. After the rehearsal it was decided that Chopin should produce it on October 11 at a concert in the theatre. This concert took place before a crowded house, and was a brilliant success. It started with a symphony by Gorner; then came the first movement of the concerto. According to custom, a song number was next inserted; it was an air with chorus by Soliva, who conducted at the concert. It was sung by a friend of Mlle. Gładkowska, Mlle. Wołków, who had made her début at the theatre a little time after her. She was dressed in blue and looked fairy-like. Then Chopin played the rest of his concerto. After an interval came the second part, consisting of the Overture to *William Tell,* then the Cavatina from the *Donna del Lago: O quante lagrime,* sung by Mlle. Gładkowska, dressed in white and crowned with roses. Lastly, Chopin was heard once more in a Fantasia on Polish airs.

This Concerto in E minor is very long, and shows more deliberate effort and less inspiration than the previous one. Niecks himself recognises this. The first movement begins, like the Concerto in F, with an orchestral introduction, but one twice as long (138 bars), composed of periods following each other in a row and stating a series of new or imitative themes — a regular table of contents. The introductory passage and the first subject are in E minor, the second subject in E major. This second subject, forming a period of 8 bars, ends with a charming surprise: the last bar leads back to the tonic through the key of C sharp minor.

The piano part itself is more monotonous than that of the concerto in F, which may be caused by the fact that the theme group and the second subject, as we have just said, are one in E minor and the other in E major. The development section starts modulating from C major; then the theme is repeated in E minor, the second subject in the relative major G, and the conclusion finally returns to E minor. The cadential group, instead of leading up to the chord of E, ends in an interrupted cadence (chord of C). The orchestra enters again on this chord, plays eight bars in C major, and finally ends with eight bars in E minor.

The second movement is a Romance in E major, of which the operatic languor seems a little insipid now. "It is sustained," writes Chopin on May 15, "in a romantic vein, tranquil and somewhat melancholy. It should produce the same impression as if the eye were resting upon a landscape grown dear to one, which calls up beautiful memories in the soul, for instance on a fine moonlight night in spring." M. Vincent d'Indy has demonstrated the ornamental character of the melody by abstracting its melodic plan and writing below it the phrase as Chopin stated and then repeated it:

The last movement is a Rondo in E major. It has this peculiarity, that the whole exposition is in C sharp minor. The orchestra first gives out a period made up of two undeveloped motives of the simplest possible kind. Next the solo repeats it in an ornamental form with a gay, well-marked rhythm. Here is the unadorned phrase as given out by the orchestra:

And here is the ornamental phrase as given out by the piano:

This period is heard twice, and once more given out in F sharp. Then a running passage ending on the dominant of E introduces fresh repetitions. A second passage for the orchestra, which is in reality no more than a fresh introduction, reintroduces a fresh recapitulation of the first period on the piano, in the form of a refrain in twelve bars. This entry of the piano has as its sole motive to interrupt for a moment the heavy orchestral statement. Immediately afterwards, the orchestra continues to present to us in E, undeveloped and in a string, a series of rhythms into which a fresh accent is only introduced by syncopations and repeated notes.

The piano next makes itself heard again and weaves brilliant arabesques around these motives. And so we come to the second subject which is, as usual, characterised by a more expressive melody. This melody is in A major. It is concluded by the orchestra a tone higher, in B, preparing for a fresh entry of the piano in this key. The effect is most graceful and characteristic.

This repetition in B minor is concluded by the piano in A; the piano passes it on to the orchestra, which ends it in F; and the phrase starts off again for the third time, this time in F. The melody is as follows:

This leads us to a *divertissement* in A major, with running passages in the left hand and a counter-melody in the right hand, which forms the cadential group. A repetition of the initial period in E flat major, then in E natural, forms the refrain, and ends this first fragment. We pass to the development section. After which the second subject alone is repeated in its entirety. Immediately afterwards begins the cadence, and a whole page of scales and arpeggi in both hands on the chord of E serves as a conclusion.

*   *   *

THE concert of October 11 was the third and last which Chopin gave at Warsaw. He left on November 1, 1830. His friends gave him a banquet at Wola, the first village on the road as you leave Warsaw. Elsner had composed a cantata which was sung by the students from the Conservatoire. They handed the traveller a silver goblet, filled with Polish earth. Chopin wept; he had a presentiment that he would never see Poland again.

NOTES TO PART ONE

[1] "I have still one foot in your house, and the other in my room, where my hostess works, and never at home at present, but rather, as is my way, in strange regions of space. Imaginary

regions, no doubt, but I am not ashamed of it: does not the Polish proverb say that imagination leads to action, and I for one am a true Mazovian" (July 20, 1845).

[2] In 1849 Sikorski (*Wspomnienie Szopena*, p. 515), followed by Karasowski, gave the wrong date, March 1, 1809, (*Friedrich Chopin*, new ed., p. 8). Yet Liszt had given the correct date (*F. Chopin*, 6th ed., p. 213). Chopin seems to have contrived to recall his age by means of a present. "It seems," says Liszt, "that the date of his birth was fixed in his memory solely by a watch presented to him in 1820 by a great artist, with the following inscription: *Madame Catalani to Frederick Chopin, at the age of ten.*"

[3] A. Szulc, *Fryderyk Chopin*, Posen, 1873, p. 15.

[4] Stanislas Leszczyński was King of Poland from 1704–1709, after which he was given the duchies of Lorraine and Bar. He reigned there till 1766.

[5] Count Wodziński, *Les trois romans de Frédéric Chopin* (Paris, 1886). "Whether he drew his origin from Nancy or whether, as some of his biographers have claimed, he was descended from one Szop, a trooper, valet or haiduk in the service of Stanislas Leszczyński, who was brought to Lorraine as a consequence of his master's adventures."

[6] This is the version given by Count Frederick Skarbek in his Memoirs; cf. F. Niecks, *Frederick Chopin*, 3rd. edition, London, 1902, I, p. 12.

[7] Nicholas Chopin's pupil, Count Frederick Skarbek, was a very distinguished man, a poet, scholar and philanthropist, and professor at the University of Warsaw. In his Memoirs he speaks of his tutor with affection and respect. Friendly relations were maintained between the two families.

[8] Louise married Joseph Calasante Jendrzejewicz, professor of administrative law at the Institute of Rural Agriculture at Marimont. Isabelle married Anthony Barcziński, who was a schoolmaster, an inspector at the Warsaw Gymnasium, and, towards 1860, director of the department of steam navigation on the Vistula. Emilienne died at the age of fourteen, in 1827.

[9] Count Wodziński, *op. cit.*, pp. 1–2.

[10] After the Revolution of 1831, Nicholas Chopin was examiner at the training school for teachers, and French master at the Catholic Clerical Academy. He died in 1844.

[11] M. Karasowski, *Friedrich Chopin*, p. 9.

[12] Zywny was born in 1756. After being court pianist to Prince Casimir Sapieha he set up as a music teacher at Warsaw. His lessons cost three florins an hour, and he amassed a fortune. He did not die until 1842.

[13] Cf. F. Niecks, *Frederick Chopin as a Man and Musician*, I, p. 31.

[14] M. Karasowski, *op. cit.*, pp. 10–11. Chopin's gift for improvisation is one of his characteristic qualities. In this he was as much a poet as a musician. There are many anecdotes current as to this. Some would have it that he calmed an uproar in his father's house by improvising at the piano a scene of robbers falling asleep in the forest. As this happened the music became so soft that the rebellious children fell asleep just like the robbers. The story is pretty, if not very credible. Chopin was fond of improvising in the dark. As he could not darken the Grand Duke's saloon, we may imagine that he fixed his eyes on the ceiling so as not to be distracted.

[15] Cf. F. Niecks, *op. cit*, I, p. 32. A pleasing anecdote is recorded as an illustration of this simplicity. He was overjoyed at the coat and collar which he wore at the concert of February 24,

1818. After he had played, his mother asked him what the public liked best. "Oh, mamma," replied the child ingenuously, "everybody was looking at my collar." M. Karasowski, *op. cit.*, pp. 9–10.

[16] A. Sowiński, *Słownik muzyków polskich* (Paris, 1874), p. 92.

[17] The only one of our contemporaries who has seen and heard Chopin, M. Ladislas Mickiewicz, remembers how, after playing the piano at his mother's house, the musician asked for a hat, and imitated in turn the Austrian Emperor, the King of Prussia and the Tsar.

[18] Franz Liszt, *F. Chopin*, p. 22.

[19] "The part of Poland where Chopin was born and brought up is inhabited by a peculiar people, the Mazovians, who are very musical. Their love of music is so great that they make songs about the most ordinary incidents of life, managing to find a charming or pathetic side in them." M. Karasowski, *Friedrich Chopin*, p. 18.

[20] Kleczyński, *Frederic Chopin* (1880), pp. 90–91.

[21] As we shall see, it is not a case of folk dances, as one sees them in Sweden or in Russia. Liszt shows him to us when quite a child, accompanying the dance of his lovely fellow-countrywomen at the piano. "There he saw displayed the chaste graces of his captivating fellow-countrywomen, who left in him an indelible memory of the spell cast by their enthusiasm, so spirited and yet so controlled, when the major key once again introduced one of those figures which none but the spirit of a chivalrous people could create and make a national possession" (*F. Chopin*, p. 218). A few pages later Liszt bears even more explicit witness to this. "In later days," he says, "Chopin was fond of telling stories about the times when he used to see the best society of Warsaw dancing at some notable and splendid fête,

before he had yet realised all the varied and profound sentiments which the melodies and rhythms of the national dances were capable of containing and expressing." (p. 221.)

[22] E. Poirée, *Chopin*, p. 71.

[23] This was not altogether Liszt's opinion. If he is to be believed, Chopin was transfigured in the country. It is true that he neither observed nor described these rustic landscapes. "Yet it was easy to see that he had a very vivid impression of them." (*F. Chopin*, p. 212.) At least, he worked more easily in the country than in Paris, and almost the whole of his works between 1839 and 1847 were written at Nohant.

[24] Musical terminology is variable. The word *motive* is here used to designate the primitive germ, most often consisting of one bar. The motives are grouped in *figures* (*incises*), the figures in *phrases*, the phrases in *periods*. The grouping normally occurs by twos, so that the figure consists of two bars, the phrase of four, the period of eight. It is this square system which is usually followed by Chopin. We shall keep the word *theme* to designate the musical idea. Cf. pp. 114, 120, etc.

[25] F. Liszt, *F. Chopin*, pp. 36–37. A. Mickiewicz has given a fine description of the Polonaise in the last canto of *Pan Tadeusz*. "Chopin," writes Liszt, "was certainly inspired several times by *Pan Tadeusz*, the scenes of which lend themselves so well to the representation of those emotions which he best liked to reproduce." (Ib. p. 46). The musician was on friendly terms with Mickiewicz, and may have interpreted his poem *Świteź* in his second Ballade. Ed. Ganche, *Dans le souvenir de Frédéric Chopin*, p. 27.

[26] We refer to Count Michael Cleophas, the last treasurer of the Grand Duchy of Lithuania, born at Gutzow in 1765, who died at Florence in 1833. Besides polonaises, he wrote songs, marches

and operas. He published four volumes entitled *Memoirs of Mikhael Oginski on Poland and the Poles* (1826–1827).

[27] Lipiński was one of the most famous violinists of the nineteenth century, and a prolific composer. He was born in 1790 at Radzin, and died at his estate of Les Aigles near Lwów in 1861.

[28] This Viennese violinist was born in 1789; he did not die until 1863, so may have read Liszt's somewhat disagreeable remark.

[29] F. Liszt, *op. cit.*, p. 50.

[1] Frederick was a delicate lad and his parents thought that a whey cure would do him good. At Reinerz the doctor forbade him to climb the Heuscheuer, as the air on top of it was too keen. A widow having died, leaving two children destitute, Chopin gave a concert for the orphans (Karasowski, p. 21). Our information about his visit comes from a letter which he wrote to Kolberg on August 28 (Niecks I, 57–58).

[2] R. Schumann, *Gesammelte Schriften*, II, p. 35.

[3] He did not fail to do so even in his last year at school, and his final examinations were not very brilliant.

[4] Sowiński (*Słownik . . .*, p. 101), who mentions Ernemann, does not know much about him, except that he was a pianist and composer who had a certain vogue as a teacher at Warsaw about 1836. As for Fryderyk Buchholtz, Sowiński says that he was one of the leading piano-makers of Warsaw. His instruments were distinguished by their beauty and volume of tone. (*ib.* p. 44).

[5] This letter was published by Karasowski, pp. 24–26. Cf. F. Hoesick, *Chopin*, I, p. 130.

[6] The manuscript of the Rondo was as early as 1831 catalogued at Vienna as a collector's piece among Aloys Fuchs' autographs. But neither of these works appeared during Chopin's life. They form part of the posthumous works edited by Fontana, the Polonaise as op. 71, the Rondo as op. 73.

[7] R. Schumann, *op. cit.*, Reclam ed., Leipzig, I, pp. 14–15.

[8] This was Adolf Martin Schlesinger, who in 1810 had founded the *Schlesingersche Buch-und Musikalienhandlung.*

[9] By Spontini.

[10] M. Karasowski, *op. cit.*, pp. 30–31.

[11] Chopin writes to Woyciechowski on Dec. 27, 1828: "The score of my Rondo in the style of a Krakowiak is finished. The introduction is as comic as I am in my winter cloak; but the trio is not yet quite finished." Karasowski, *op. cit.*, p. 36.

[12] R. Schumann, *op. cit.*, I, pp. 187–188.

[1] "It was very interesting to me to become personally known to Gyrowetz, Lachner, Kreutzer and Seyfried; above all, I had long talks with Mayseder," writes Chopin to his parents on August 12.

[2] This tune, in mazurka rhythm, is sung at weddings.

[3] Letter of September 12, 1829, to Titus Woyciechowski. M. Karasowski, *op. cit.*, p. 60 *sq.*

[4] "It is said here almost unanimously that I play too softly, or rather, too tenderly, for the public. They are used to the big drum of the virtuosi. . . . But I had rather they said I was too gentle than too violent." Letter of August 12 to his parents.

[5] This work was not published till 1854; Klengel died at Dresden on November 22, 1852.

[6] Letter of August 26, 1829. The Polish text is in Hoesick, *Chopin* I, p. 174. The German translation given by Karasowski, *op. cit.*, p. 54–55, is a little different.

[1] M. Karasowski, *op. cit.*, pp. 65–66.

[2] F. Niecks, *Frederick Chopin*, I, p. 200.

[3] It was published among his posthumous works, op. 71.

[4] *Leszek Biały.*

[5] F. Niecks, *Frederick Chopin*, I, pp. 208–209.

[6] Elsner's overture was replaced by a symphony of Nowakowski's; and Gorner's divertissement by an *Air varié* of de Bériot, played by Bielawski.

[7] This time it was an air from *Helen and Malvina*, by Soliva, professor of singing at the Warsaw Conservatoire.

PART TWO

EARLY YEARS IN PARIS

1831–1837

CHAPTER 1

CHOPIN went first to Vienna. He was joined at the frontiers of Poland, at Kalisch, by his friend Titus Woyciechowski, who was a little older than himself, a great music-lover and a good pianist. They arrived at Breslau on November 6, 1830, at Dresden on the 12th; passing through Prague they went to Vienna, where they arrived at the end of the month.

Their stay in Vienna was full of disappointments. Of their old friends, Blahetka was at Stuttgart; others were dead or ill or indifferent. Czerny asked him most politely whether he had worked well. Titus had hardly arrived when he returned to Poland to take part in the insurrection which had broken out on November 29. Chopin was not strong enough, and his parents begged him to stay in Austria, so he renounced the idea of following Titus; but he afterwards changed his mind, tried to join him, failed to do so, and returned to Vienna. It was very painful to him to be absent from his country during this tragic year. Karasowski informs us that many of his letters belonging to this period were prudently destroyed by their recipient. And he points out how many of those which have survived are very bitter. Those addressed to his parents, however, have a pretence of gaiety. He evidently desires to reassure his people, and Niecks wisely warns us only to trust these letters with reservations.

Far from Poland, far from his own people, far from his beloved, Chopin was to experience yet further trials in Vienna. Powerful persons attempted to exploit him. In 1830 Haslinger, the publisher, had brought out the Variations on *La ci darem la mano,* which had had so much success the year before, and deposited the manuscript at the Imperial Library, where Chopin had the pleasant surprise of finding it. But in order to obtain more works for nothing, Haslinger affected to treat them as trifles. Chopin, for his part, had taken as his motto: " Pay, brute! " They did not succeed in coming to an agreement, and Chopin's manuscripts remained in Haslinger's hands unpublished until the musician's death. It was for this reason that the Sonata in C minor and the Variations in E major on a German air, which were left with Haslinger, one in 1828 and the other in 1830, did not appear till 1851. The same unpleasantnesses occurred when he was looking for a hall. Du-

THE YOUTHFUL CHOPIN
From a drawing made in 1828

FRÉDÉRIC CHOPIN
From a lithograph by Vigneron, 1833

port, the new director of the Kärtnertor Theatre, was a retired dancer and very mean. " He received me very politely," writes Chopin on December 21, " for perhaps he supposes that I shall play for nothing. He is mistaken."

Chopin occupied a large room, which he rented for 30 florins a month, on the fourth floor of a house belonging to the young and kindly Baroness Lachmanowicz. This house is near the Opera House, in a fine street. The room " has three windows," he writes, " the bed is opposite, my wonderful piano is on the right, the sofa on the left; between the windows is a looking-glass, and in the middle of the room a fine big round mahogany table; the floor is polished. . . . In the morning the man-servant, who is intolerably stupid, wakes me early. I get up, my coffee is brought me, I play . . . and I often eat my breakfast cold. About nine o'clock, my German master arrives; then I usually play; thereupon Hummel [1] comes to work at my portrait, and Nidecki to study my concerto.[2] I do all this in my dressing-gown till midday, when a very nice German, a certain Leibenfrost, who works at the law-courts, arrives, and I take a walk with him on the fortifications, then I lunch wherever I am invited, or else at the inn *Zur böhmischen Köchin,* which is frequented by the

University students. We then go to one of the best cafés, as is the custom here. After that I go visiting. I return at nightfall, have my hair dressed, put on evening shoes and go to some evening party. About eleven o'clock or midnight, but never later, I come home, play, laugh, cry, read, go to bed and dream of you."

Such is his outward life; now for his deeper life. His friend John Matuszyński[3] had sent him news of Constantia. Chopin answered him on Christmas morning. He recalls how the year before, at the same time, he was in the Bernardine church — no doubt the one attended by Mlle. Gładkowska; now he is alone, in his night clothes; he kisses a ring which she gave him, and writes: "What joy is always caused me by news of my angel of peace! How I should love to touch every string of the lyre, not only those which evoke stormy emotions, but those in which are echoed the songs whose dying echoes still wander on the banks of the Danube, the songs sung by the soldiers of John Sobieski!" In order to compose these songs, Matuszyński urges him to select a poet. He answers that he is an irresolute creature, and that his choice is always a bad one. He would like to return to Warsaw, but does not wish to be a burden to his father. "I am bored with all these dinners, evening parties, concerts and balls, into which I am plunged up to the neck. I am sad, and feel myself so isolated and abandoned here. . . . But I cannot live in the way I should like. I have to dress, put on evening shoes, arrange my hair and appear in people's drawing-rooms with a smiling face; but when I get back to my room, I thunder at the piano. . . ."

His letters are charming, spontaneous confidences, reproducing the varying movements of his mind like music itself. A thousand emotions of every shade are to be seen reflected in them. Chopin is melancholy in solitude, but gay in society. He sees the Hussarzewskis, the Rzewuskis, the Beyers (Mme. Beyer is also called Constantia; what happiness to hold in his hand a handkerchief with that initial!) and a host of others. Niecks enumerates forty connections which he has made and which he mentions. But he misses his friends, and complains that he has not a soul in whom he can confide wholly. German voices produce a harsh and grating impression upon him. He loves Constantia, but has not written to her. He vacillates between adoration and doubt. He overwhelmes his friend with messages for her, and these messages are couched in two different ways: one in case she laughs at him, the other in case she asks after him kindly.[4] How young it all is! How touching, melancholy and desperately tender-hearted!

"I should like to die for you, for you all! Why am I condemned to remain here alone and abandoned?"

As always, there was excellent music at Vienna. Dr. Malfatti, who had attended Beethoven, asked Chopin to his house, and had Polish dishes cooked for him. Chopin has left a charming description of one of these little musical parties, at which he accompanied the quartet from *Moses*. It was the Feast of St. John (June 24, 1831), the doctor's name-day. "A great many people listened to our concert on the terrace outside the house. The moonlight was wonderful, the fountains played, the air was fragrant with perfume from the orangery. It was indeed an enchanting night, and the surroundings were magnificent. You can hardly imagine what a fine saloon it was in which the singing took place. The lofty windows open from top to bottom on to the terrace, from which one sees the whole of Vienna. Plenty of mirrors, little light. . . . The candour and courtesy of our host, the gay, elegant company, and the excellent supper kept us there till late."

He was made much of, but found neither a publisher nor a concert-hall. Is it surprising that his criticisms have a touch of satire? Haslinger the publisher had just brought out Hummel's last mass: "For he now lives by and for Hummel," writes Chopin to Elsner on

January 26, 1831. "It is said, however, that Hummel's last compositions are not selling, and that he paid a high price for them. That is why he sets aside all other manuscripts, and prints nothing but Strauss's things." And how could Chopin fail to be chagrined at the success of Thalberg, who was two years younger than himself? "Thalberg plays excellently," he writes, "but he is not the man for me. He is younger than I am, is liked by the ladies, makes up *pots-pourris* on *La Muette*, produces his *fortes* and *pianos* by the pedal and not by the fingers, stretches tenths as easily as I do octaves and wears diamond studs. Moscheles has no surprises for him, so it is not surprising that he likes only the tutti of my concerto. He also writes concertos." Chopin is more fully in sympathy with the violinist Sławik, who died in 1833, and Merk the violoncellist. He writes about Sławik on December 25, 1830, in the following terms: "With the exception of Paganini, I have never heard a violinist like Sławik. Ninety-six staccato notes in one length of the bow! It is almost incredible. When I had heard him, I wanted to go back home and sketch out some variations for piano and violin on an Adagio of Beethoven." But at this juncture he went to the post, and the direction of his ideas was changed, so the tears brought to his eyes by this heavenly theme bedewed Matuszyński's letter. As for Merk, Chopin heard him at the house of Fuchs, the collector who possessed the manuscript of the Rondo for two pianos. " People stayed till midnight," writes Chopin, " for Merk took it into his head to play his variations with me. He told me that he liked playing with me, and it is always a great pleasure to me to play with him. I think we go well together. He is the first violoncellist whom I have really admired."

In the spring he was resolved to leave Vienna, where he had been unable to give a single concert. But it was hard for Poles to get passports. The one he had had was mislaid. At last he received another, stipulating that he should go to London by way of Paris. On July 20, 1831, he left Vienna.

What did he write at Vienna? The three Ecossaises which appear among the posthumous works as op. 72, a number of Etudes which were published in 1833, some Mazurkas, and probably the Grand Polonaise (op. 22), which was published in 1836. It was possibly a concerto planned at Vienna which he turned later on into the Allegro de Concert, (op. 46).

By way of Linz and Salzburg he arrived at Munich, where he gave a morning concert (*Mittagsconcert*) on August 28 in the Philharmonic Society's hall. He played the Concerto in E minor, the one which had been heard at his last concert in Warsaw. The review *Flora* had a notice of it on the 30th, which gives a good characterisation both of the man and his work. It said of the pianist that: " Side by side with a finished technique, we particularly noticed a charming delicacy of execution, and an interpretation which was both beautiful and well suited to the motives. The composition was, on the whole, well and brilliantly written, without astonishing one by any extraordinary novelty or particular depth, with the exception of the Rondo, the principal idea of which, as well as the florid passage in the middle, offers a peculiar charm, due to the combination of a dash of melancholy with a whimsical fancy, thanks to which it was much liked."

The journalist added that Chopin concluded his concert with a Fantasia on Polish airs. " There is something about Slav songs," he said, " which hardly ever fails of its effect. It is difficult to discover and express the cause, for it is not only the rhythm and the frequent change from the minor to the major key which produce this charm." [5]

The critic remarked a similar blend of popular themes and brilliant caprices in the works of Bernhard Romberg, and the comparison is interesting, for Romberg was one of the first to introduce Slav music into Europe. He was a violoncellist, born in 1767, one of a regular clan of musicians who were natives of Münster. The disaster of 1806 had driven him from Berlin, where he was solo violoncellist at the Chapel Royal, and between then and 1815 he went on a number of concert tours in Austria, Russia and Sweden. His works include four collections of Russian melodies for violoncello and orchestra, Swedish, Spanish and Roumanian melodies and some Polish ones. He was one of the inventors of local colour in music. At the time when Chopin was in Munich he had himself retired to Hamburg. He was sixty-three years old. He made another tour to London and Paris in 1839; he died at Hamburg in 1841.

The Poles, fired with dreams of national resurrection, urged on their fellow-countryman in his search for a national art. Shortly before he left Vienna, Stephen Witwicki wrote to him: "You really ought to be the creator of Polish opera; I am deeply convinced that you might be, and that you could become a national composer, and discover an extremely rich vein of expression which would bring you no common renown. Provided that you always keep in view nationality, nationality, and once again nationality. . . . There is a native melody, just as there is a native climate. The mountains, the forests, the water and the plains have a native, inward voice. I am convinced that a Slav opera, called into existence by a composer rich in emotion and ideas, will shine one day like a new sun in the musical world. . . . If you go to Italy, you would do well to stop for a time in Dalmatia and Illyria, to get to know the songs of this sister race, and also in Moravia and Bohemia. Search for popular Slav melodies, as a mineralogist searches for rocks and metals in the mountains and valleys. Perhaps you may even think fit to write down certain songs. . . ."

The political hopes of Poland were to be cruelly annihilated. From Munich Chopin betook himself to Stuttgart. It was here that on September 8, 1831, he heard of the capture of Warsaw by the Russians. It is said that it was in his grief for this catastrophe that he composed the magnificent Etude in C minor.

From Stuttgart Chopin went on to Paris at the end of September. In spite of his passport, which said " Passing through Paris to London," he was to live and die in France.

CHAPTER 2

When Chopin arrived in Paris in the autumn of 1831, it was in a fever of excitement. He described with disgust a demonstration which he witnessed: "I cannot tell you," he writes to Titus Woyciechowski, "what an unpleasant impression was produced upon me by the horrible voices of these rioters and by this disaffected mob." The amusing thing is that the demonstration had been held in honour of Poland.

The early years of the July Monarchy were accompanied by a magnificent bloom of art. In 1831 Lamartine began to write *Jocelyn.* Victor Hugo published the *Feuilles d'Automne* and *Notre-Dame de Paris,* Balzac *La Peau de Chagrin;* Eugène Sue *Atar Gull;* in 1830 Musset had produced the *Contes d'Espagne et d'Italie.* He was in mourning for his father, whom he had lost on April 7, 1831, and was writing *La Coupe et les Lèvres* and *A quoi rêvent les jeunes filles,* which were to be published together in 1832 as *Le Spectacle dans un fauteuil.* Gautier brought out his collection of *Poésies* in 1830, and produced *Albertus* in 1833. Musset and Gautier were within a few months of Chopin's age. It was in this year 1831, too, that George Sand settled in Paris, contributed her first articles to the *Figaro* and the *Revue de Paris,* and published at the end of the year her first novel: *Rose et Blanche.* During the summer she wrote *Indiana,* which was to appear in May, 1832.

At the Théâtre-Français, where Taylor was commissary royal, it must be admitted that the year had been very lacking in lustre; out of the sixteen works produced for the first time, not one has left any record for posterity, either of itself or of its author. The year 1832 was to be more brilliant, with *Le Roi s'amuse* by Victor Hugo (November 22) and Casimir Delavigne's *Louis XI* (February 9).

At the Odéon 1831 was a memorable year. After the failure of Musset's *Nuit vénitienne* (December 1, 1830), the theatre had closed on December 10; but on January 11, 1831, it gave *Napoléon Bonaparte* by Dumas, on April 25, *Norma ou l'Infanticide* by Soumet, on June 25 Vigny's *La Maréchale d'Ancre,* on October 20 *Charles VII chez ses grands vassaux,* by Dumas, not to mention forty works less worthy to be recalled.

The Vaudeville, the Gymnase, the Variétés and the Palais-Royal were abundantly provided for by a number of comic dramatists, including Scribe, Melesville, Saintine, Ancelot, Duvert, Lausanne, Dumersan, Brazier, Desvergers, Desnoyers, Bayard and Anicet-Bourgeois. At the Nouveautés sometimes dramas were played, sometimes vaudevilles, and even *drames-vaudevilles,* such as Ancelot's *Le château de Saint-Bris* (July 13). At the Gaîté, managed by Pixérécourt, drama and melodrama were triumphant; the same was the case at the Ambigu. The Porte St. Martin, where Frederick Lemaître, Bocage and Mlle. Georges were acting, and which was one of the strongholds of romanticism, played *Antony* by Dumas on May 3, Escousse's *Farruch le Maure* on June 25, Hugo's *Marion Delorme* on August 11, and Dinaux and Dumas' *Richard Darlington* on December 10.

The Salon of 1831 had been quite an event. There had been far more pictures than at the previous Salon, which had been that of 1827.[1] Delacroix had sent six pictures, one of which was the famous *28 juillet* (Liberty leading the people), now in the Louvre.[2] Visitors all paused before *Les Enfants d'Edouard* (The Princes in the Tower) by Paul Delaroche, and before his portrait of Mlle. Sontag.[3] Deveria, who had shown his *Birth of Henri IV* at the previous Salon, had this time an official painting representing *The King's Oath at the*

Chamber of Deputies, August 9, 1830; his other exhibits were a *Death of Jeanne d'Arc,* a figure of a courtier of the period of Louis XIII, a portrait of a woman, and lastly two pictures which, like Delacroix's *Richelieu,* formed part of a vast series ordered for the Palais-Royal: one represented Cardinal Retz on the Day of the Barricades, the other a ball given in honour of Christian VII in 1768. The pendant to Deveria's picture, namely, Anne of Austria's answer to Cardinal Retz, had been executed by Ary Scheffer.[4] "The admirable and naïve compositions of M. Decamps, which are unexampled anywhere,"[5] Lethière's *Virginius,* which had been talked about for twenty years, Isabey's *View of Dunkirk* and Huet's landscapes. Horace Vernet had a *Leo XII* and a *Judith.* Hersent exhibited the portraits of the King, the Queen and the Duc de Montpensier; Champmartin, the portraits of the Duc de Fitzjames, the Duc de Crussol, Mmes. de Mirbel and de Mennechet. Decaisne, who copied the style of Lawrence, sent a portrait of Malibran and one of the Duke of Orleans. Dubufe touched the hearts of the bourgeois with *The Nest, The Tomtit* and *The Alsatian Girl.* "It is not even bad painting," said Gustave Planche in disgust. Sigalon sent a *St. Jerome* and a *Christ.* Lastly, there were the painters who had taken refuge in Italy,

Léopold Robert and Schnetz. The former exhibited a Neapolitan woman "weeping over the ruins of her house, destroyed by an earthquake," some young girls, some pifferari, an *Insurrection at Cività Castellana* and a *Burial in Rome.*[6] The latter had designed for St. Etienne du Mont his *Sufferers imploring the help of the Virgin.* His Italian pictures represented peasants surprised by the floods of the Tiber, young girls bathing in the Lake of Nemi, and a woman of the Roman Campagna frightened by a bull.[7]

Paris had never been more definitely a musical capital than in 1831. The opera *La Marquise de Brinvilliers,* played in 1831 at the Opéra-Comique, was the joint work of nine fashionable musicians: Cherubini, aged seventy-one, the Nestor of Music; Auber, Batton, Berton, Boieldieu, Blangini, Carafa, Herold and Paer. Berlioz, who had won the Prix de Rome in the previous year, did not return to Paris till 1832.

The opera had Véron as its director and Habeneck as its conductor. The stars were Mme. Damoreau (1826), Mme. Dorus (1830), Cornélie Falcon (born in 1812 and engaged in 1831), who had just created the part of Alice, and whose career was so short; among the men, Nourrit, Dabadie, Levasseur and Derivis.

On April 6, 1831, they played Weber's *Euryanthe,* with

the words of Castilblaze, on June 20 *Le Philtre,* a one-act piece by Auber, with words by Scribe, on July 18 *L'Orgie,* a ballet by Carafa,[8] with a scenario by Scribe and Coralli, and lastly, on November 21, *Robert the Devil* by Meyerbeer, with words by Scribe and Germain Delavigne. The *Almanach des spectacles,* which has a whole series of marks for the works which it mentions, marks all of these with an S, signifying "success." [9]

Robert the Devil had made a sensation. Meyerbeer was a pupil of the Abbé Vogler, who had initiated him into the scholastic forms of music, and was later an imitator of the Italians. He had been kept away from the theatre by mourning for more than two years. His new work combined the Italian with the German style. "He blends together these two styles, these different kinds of colour, wedding with rare felicity Weber and Rossini, Italy and Germany." [10]

The Italian theatre was managed by Rossini and Robert, and had as its conductor Zamboni. In 1831 it had given only one novelty, Guecco's *Prova d'un opera seria* (January 6). But the company was a splendid one. Among the principal tenors were the two Rubinis, Gianbattista and Giacomo; among the principal basses, Tamburini; Lablache had come to Paris in 1830. Of the women, Pasta had almost given up singing since 1829; Malibran divided her time between London and Paris; Giulia Grisi did not come to Paris till 1832, Carlotta Ungher till 1833.

The Opéra-Comique had as its conductor Valentino, and on May 3 played Herold's *Zampa, or the Marble Betrothed*, with words by Melesville; two comic operas by Adam, *Le Morceau d'ensemble* (March 7) and *Le Grand Prix* (July 9), a work of Carafa's, *Le Livre de l'Ermite* (August 11), and a few works of minor importance.

In 1828 an event had taken place the importance of which has been considerable in the history of music. This was the foundation, by a decree of February 15, 1828, of the *Société des Concerts du Conservatoire.*

" It was to one of the last Ministers of the Household of King Charles X, the Vicomte Sosthène de la Rochefoucauld, that France owes the foundation of the Conservatoire concerts. It was on the petition of Habeneck, and at the request of Cherubini, that the noble Viscount obtained the memorable decree, which was to regenerate French music." Such are the words of Elwart, who has recorded the history of the *Société des concerts.* And he defines Habeneck's plan as follows: " The noble motive which prompted the elder Habeneck was the desire to make known the symphonic masterpieces of Haydn, Mozart and above all, of Beethoven. This great artist, whose heart was as generous as his character was elevated, while respecting the dignity of the programmes of the Society's concerts, so managed things that side by side with the works of the greatest masters should figure the as yet unknown works of their young and studious rivals." [11]

The first concert took place on March 9, 1828. In 1831 the Society gave seven concerts. The first took place on January 30, for the benefit of those wounded during the July Days. Perhaps music-lovers may find a certain interest in seeing these old programmes. The concert of January 30 included Beethoven's *Eroica* Symphony, an air from *Robin des Bois* (a French version of *Der Freischütz*) sung by Mlle. Dorus, a portion of Beethoven's Septet, a chorus from *Euryanthe*, an Air with variations for flute, oboe, horn and bassoon, by the flautist Tulou; the trio from Act II of *William Tell*, sung by the artists who had created it at the opera in 1829, Nourrit, Dabadie and Levasseur, a piano solo composed and performed by Kalkbrenner, and lastly, the overture to *Oberon*.

The second concert, on February 13, began with Beethoven's Symphony in A; next came a duet of Carafa's, a theme with variations for violoncello by Ditzand, played by Vaslin, an air from Boieldieu, *Deux Nuits*, the finale from *Fidelio* and the overture to *Euryanthe*. The third concert, on February 27, included the *Prometheus* overture, a fantasia for clarinet and bassoon performed by Butteux and Henry, a chorus of Beethoven's, a Rondo for violin by Habeneck, played by his pupil Alard, then aged sixteen, a scene from Gluck's *Orpheus* and Beethoven's C minor Symphony.

At the fourth concert, on March 13, were heard the Pastoral Symphony, an air of Rossini's, a flute solo by Dorus,[12] the sextet from *Don Giovanni,* a violin solo by Kreutzer, played by his pupil Massart, the quartet from Méhul's *Irato* and the overture to *Robin des Bois*.

At the fifth concert, on March 26, the Society played the Choral Symphony for the first time; with it were performed the overture to *Fidelio,* an air sung by Mlle. Dorus, and a bassoon solo played by Wilbert.

At the sixth concert, on April 10, were heard a symphony by Onslow, an air by Mercadante, an organ piece by Mme. Louise de * * *, *née* Rousseau, professor of harmony at the Conservatoire, a duet from *Armide,* a violoncello solo by Romberg, the finale from *Fidelio* and the *König Stephan* overture.

Lastly, at the seventh concert, on April 24, they repeated the Symphonies in A and in C minor, and the scene in the underworld from *Orpheus,* with the addition of a concerto by Rode and an air by Pacini.

The condition of instrumental music is recorded for us by Fétis, whose articles on " The Present State of Music in France " appeared in *L'Europe littéraire* for 1833. From the fourth article, which appeared on April 9, I draw the following information:

The fashionable style of piano-playing at the beginning of the Revolution had been that of Steibelt,[13] who had settled in Paris about that time. " This style consisted in a cantabile style for the right hand, the left hand executing a vigorous accompaniment of chords." Steibelt's rival was Hermann. Adam began to make a reputation about the same time. Of his pupils, several of whom became famous, the most celebrated was Kalkbrenner, " the most amazing pianist of our day, both for brilliance of execution and correct technique." Fétis further mentions Mme. de Montgeroult, the teacher who formed Pradher, who was appointed a professor at the Conservatoire when hardly more than a child. " The fault for which he might possibly be blamed was that of banging the keys instead of touching them lightly: this fault has become characteristic of his school; it must even be confessed that it is that of almost all French pianists. In the first rank among the pupils of Pradher, may be noted M. Henri Herz, who for about ten years past has modified his talent in accordance with the systems of German pianists, and is particularly distinguished for his skill in striking the most widely separated notes with a rapidity which is sometimes almost miraculous. Finally, among the professors who have produced the greatest number of piano pupils we must place M. Zimmermann, who has been a professor at the Conservatoire for more than fifteen years." [14]

Compositions for the piano had undergone a regrettable change during the last twenty-five years. " Sonatas and other works in classical and regular forms have disappeared, and made way for pieces of fancywork, consisting of well-known themes and operatic airs with adornments; all these are known as fantasias or *airs variés,* though nothing could be less fantastic or varied. The form of these pieces always seems to be copied from the same pattern. All inventive merit seems to have almost entirely disappeared, and as regards skill in writing, most of them are worthy of no respect. Steibelt was the first pianist to introduce this kind of piece into France; it was easy to foresee the ruin of good piano music by the favour with which they were received in general society; and indeed it has not been slow in coming, for these frivolous arrangements are nowadays the only things in vogue among pianists. The monotony of these publications is only interrupted by a few concertos, show pieces for use at big concerts."

The violin school was represented by Kreutzer and Baillot,[15] and, thanks to them, was a very brilliant one. "The French school of violinists," writes Fétis, "has become the first in Europe. Hence the ability of our orchestras. Our basses," he adds, "are also remarkable for their skill." And he mentions "among those who are distinguishing themselves today M. Norblin, and, above all, young Franchome (*sic*), whose talent will one day be among the most celebrated in Europe."

Wind instruments were unequal in quality. French clarinettists lacked the mellifluous tone of German artists. Their flautists, on the contrary, were famous for beauty of tone and elegance of execution. "Tulou and Drouet in particular, in their different styles, have risen to a degree of skill which has not been surpassed by any artist in foreign countries." The same may be said of the oboe, as played by the virtuoso Brod. "M. Brod is a pupil of Vogt, and equals his master in the most important qualities, perhaps surpassing him in the delicacy of his playing; it is noticed, however, that he is less faultless in the execution of difficult passages." Lastly, there was a very promising bassoon-player, Vollent.

Chopin was enchanted with what he heard. "Only here," he writes to Elsner, "can one learn what singing is." And to Woyciechowski he says: "I have never known such fine execution as in the *Barber of Seville* at the Italian opera, with Lablache, Rubini and Malibran-Garcia in the leading parts. . . . You cannot imagine what Lablache is like. Some say that Pasta's voice is getting weaker, but I have never heard such a divine voice in my life. Malibran covers a range of three octaves with her marvellous voice; her singing is unique and enchanting in its style. That excellent tenor Rubini executes an unending series of roulades — which are often too brilliant — vibrates and trills incessantly, which is hailed with applause. He possesses an incomparable voice. Mme. Damoreau Cinti also sings admirably; I prefer her singing to Malibran's. . . . The latter astounds, but Cinti charms. She sings chromatic runs with a perfection of *coloratura* almost as great as when Tulou, the famous flautist, plays them." Chopin's lodgings were at 27, Boulevard Poissonnière, on the fourth storey. He had a letter of introduction to Paer from Malfatti. Paer introduced him to Cherubini, at whose house the whole musical world met every Monday. "During recent years," writes Véron, "one might often meet at his house Hummel, Liszt, Chopin, Moscheles, Mme. Grassini and Mme. Falcon, then young and brilliant, both in talent and in beauty; Auber and Halévy, the master's favourite pupils, Meyerbeer and Rossini."

The prince of pianists was Kalkbrenner. He was at that time forty-seven years old. He was a tall, stiff man, with regular features and a smiling, rather ironical mouth, extremely polished manners and the air of a diplomatist. His playing was smooth, sustained and harmonious, not seeking after an effect of power, but delightful in its sonority of tone and perfect in its evenness, pure rather than impassioned in style, and based exclusively upon finger-work. For this work, Kalkbrenner had invented the "hand-guide," that is to say, a bar of wood parallel with the keyboard, upon which the wrist was supported. This support to the wrist preserved a perfect elasticity, while the fingers not only acquired firmness, but learnt to produce the required quality of sound by themselves alone. Kalkbrenner was the master of Stamaty, who taught Saint-Saëns.

Kalkbrenner praised Chopin's style and touch; he

compared them to the style of Cramer and the touch of Field. It was magnificent praise. Field was undoubtedly the most delightful pianist of the day. When he came to Paris in 1832 Fétis wrote about him: " Anyone who has not heard this great pianist can have no idea of his finger technique, which is such that the greatest difficulties appear quite simple, while his hand appears perfectly steady. Moreover, he is no less astounding in the art with which he attacks the note, with an infinite variation in the different shades of strength, sweetness and accent." As for Jean-Baptiste Cramer, he was one of the greatest pianists of all time. Yet Kalkbrenner's praise was subject to certain reservations. All his contemporaries recognised that Chopin's technique was excellent; but it was not the result of assiduous practice. His father writes to him: " You know that the technique of playing has not taken up much of your time, and that your mind has been more employed than your fingers. Others have passed whole days working at the keyboard, but you have rarely spent a whole hour practising the works of others."

It is possible that the impeccable Kalkbrenner discovered some flaws in his technique. According to Kleczyński he was scandalised at the boldness of Chopin's fingering. However that may be, he offered to give the young musician lessons for three years; thanks to which he would be able to perpetuate the grand school of piano-playing.

Chopin was dubious about it, and consulted his family. His father merely recommended him to think it over, to wait, and to be cautious. But his sister Louise sent him, on November 27, 1831, a very long letter describing the indignation of Elsner, who judged Kalkbrenner's motive to be an interested one. We may judge in our turn that Elsner's indignation was that of a rival teacher. However that may be, he had communicated his wrath to the family, who had nevertheless at first greeted Kalkbrenner's proposition with joy. In his fury Elsner said some excellent things, which Louise repeated: " Elsner does not want you to imitate, and he puts it very well, saying that no imitation is as good as originality; so soon as you imitate, you cease to be original. . . ." And, further on: " Elsner maintains . . . that you . . . must make your own way: your genius will guide you. Here is another thing he said: ' Frederick has drawn from his native soil that trait of his originality which consists in rhythm . . . and the fact that his thoughts have unusual nobility renders him all the more original and characteristic.' He does not want you to lose this." Finally, he wanted Chopin to be no mere executant, but a composer. His place was between Rossini and Mozart. He wanted him to go beyond piano music and achieve opera. Like others, he hoped that Chopin would found a Polish national opera, and he urged him, if an opportunity offered, to depict the insurrection of 1831 on the stage.[16]

It must be added that in his answer to Chopin, who had written to consult him directly, Elsner is much more circumspect. He expresses himself merely in general terms, and urges his pupil to devote himself to the art of music rather than to technique. Chopin answered him on December 14. He enumerated the reasons which induced him to choose the career of a pianist. He defended Kalkbrenner against the suspicions of his Warsaw master. " I do not wish to learn the art of the piano in Germany," he said, " for nobody there could tell me what I am particularly lacking in. I could not see the beam in my eye myself. It is far too much to study for three years: Kalkbrenner realised this himself when he had heard me more often. You may see from this, dear M. Elsner, that the sentiment of envy is foreign to a true and worthy virtuoso. I should certainly have decided to study for another three years, if I were certain of attaining by that means the object which I have set before me. What is evident to me is that I shall never be a copy of Kalkbrenner; he will be powerless to turn aside my intention, which may be bold, but is a noble one: namely, to found a new epoch in art." [17]

The upshot of it was that Chopin took a few lessons from Kalkbrenner, but found a pretext for not continuing them. They remained friends. Chopin dedicated the Concerto in E minor to Kalkbrenner, and Kalkbrenner composed some Variations brillantes upon a mazurka by Chopin.

Better still, Kalkbrenner helped Chopin to organise his first concert. He had introduced him to Camille Pleyel. It was in Pleyel's Rooms, at 9, Rue Cadet, that Chopin was first heard on January 26, 1832. The audience was not very large: some Poles and a few French people who received cards of invitation. The receipts did not cover the expenses.

In the first part Chopin played his Concerto in F minor, and in the second, the Variations on *La ci darem la mano*. Moreover, he took part in a strange piece by Kalkbrenner, a march followed by a polonaise for two pianos, accompanied by four others. " Is it not a mad idea? " wrote Chopin to Titus on December 16. " One of the grand pianos is a very big one — that is Kalkbrenner's; the other is a little one — that is mine. The others, which are big ones, and as loud as an orchestra, will be played on by Hiller, Osborne, Stamaty and Sowiński." [18]

Fétis reported the concert in the *Revue musicale* for March 3. After complaining that pianists' music had been composed in conventional forms which had not varied for the last thirty years, he pointed out in what the young composer's originality consisted. "Here is a young man," he said, "who, by giving himself up to his natural impressions, and following no model, has discovered, if not an absolute revolution in piano music, at least something of what composers have been seeking in vain for a long time past, namely, an abundance of original ideas whose type is nowhere to be found. This is not to say that M. Chopin is gifted with a nature as mighty as that of Beethoven, nor that there are in his music the powerful conceptions to be remarked in that great man. . . . M. Chopin was heard . . . in a concerto which caused his audience as much astonishment as pleasure, due both to the novelty of the melodic ideas and to the running passages, modulations and general structure of his pieces. There is soul in his melodies, imagination in his characteristic devices, and originality in the whole. With the merits which I have just indicated are mingled certain faults:

an excessive luxuriance of modulation and a lack of regularity in the transition from one phrase to another, so that one sometimes seems to be listening to an improvisation rather than to written music. But these faults are due to the artist's youth: they will disappear when he has gained experience. . . . As an executant this young artist is also worthy of praise. His execution is elegant, easy and graceful, and possesses both brilliance and finish. He draws only a small volume of tone from the instrument, resembling in this respect the majority of German pianists."

CHAPTER 3

"We ascended to the second floor of a little lodging-house, and I found myself face to face with a pale, melancholy, elegant young man with a slight foreign accent, brown eyes of incomparable softness and limpidity, chestnut hair almost as long as that of Berlioz and falling in a wisp on to his brow. . . . It was Chopin, who had arrived in Paris a few days before. . . . His person, his playing and his works were in such harmony that it seemed as if they could no more be separated than the different features of the same face. The tone, so peculiarly his own, which he drew from the piano was like the glance of his eye; the somewhat morbid delicacy of his nature was akin to the poetic melancholy of his nocturnes; and the care and choiceness with which he was dressed enabled one to understand the almost modish elegance of certain parts of his works; the effect which he produced upon me was, as it were, that of a natural son of Weber by a duchess."

This is how Legouvé describes Chopin, whom Berlioz had taken him to visit. The portrait drawn by Liszt is less enhanced by literary effect, but more accurate, less artificial and more truthful: "His whole person was harmonious. His glance was intelligent rather than dreamy; his soft, shrewd smile had no touch of bitterness. The fineness and transparency of his complexion charmed the eye, his fair hair was silky, his nose slightly aquiline, his movements well-bred, and his maners bore such an aristocratic stamp that one involuntarily treated him like a prince. His gestures were frequent and graceful. His voice was always toneless, and often indistinct; he was not very tall, and was slightly built. . . ."

In Paris Chopin met a great number of his fellow-countrymen who had had to leave their country after the victory of the Russians. At the beginning of 1832 they founded a literary society (*Towarzystwo Literackie*), of which Chopin became a member in 1833.[1] Among the founders of it was his intimate friend Albert Grzymala, who was the secretary. He also knew the three Counts Plater, one of whom, Ludwik Plater, the castellan, was the first vice-president of the society; he knew Karol Hofmann, who was also a member of the secretariate.[2]

By a natural reaction, political sympathy and the presence of the refugees had made Polish art fashionable. Thus in 1833 one of these refugees, the writer Karol

Forster, published a translation of the Historical Songs of Niemcewicz [3] in collaboration with French poets, illustrators and musicians. It is possible that Chopin profited by this enthusiasm for his country.

His reputation was made within a few months of his arrival. It appears that Prince Valentin Radziwill introduced him to the great world at an evening party to which he took him, we do not know where. The wife of Marshal Lannes was one of his earliest patronesses. He writes to Dominic Dziawolowski: " I belong to the highest society; I have my appointed place amongst ambassadors, princes and ministers, without myself knowing how I got there. . . ." He had many pupils. " I have to give five lessons in a morning. But do you think I am making my fortune? My carriage and my white gloves, without which I should not be as a gentleman should, cost me more than my lessons bring in."

He had left the Boulevard Poissonnière for the Cité Bergère (no. 4). He did not stay there long, but went to live at 5, Rue de la Chaussée d'Antin. His friend Matuszyński, who had served as surgeon-major in the Polish army, and had just been appointed professor at the Paris School of Medicine, came to live with him. " I cannot tell you," writes Matuszyński to his brother-in-law, " how happy we were to meet again after a separation of five years. He has become tall and broad, and I hardly recognised him. Chopin is now the leading pianist here; he gives a number of lessons, the price of which is not less than twenty francs. He has composed a great deal, and his works are much sought after." Another friend of Chopin's, Orlowski, writes: " Chopin is well and strong; he is turning the heads of all the women; the men are jealous of him. He is the fashion. No doubt we shall soon be wearing gloves *à la Chopin*. But he is consumed with longing for his country."

He did not appear much at concerts, which he disliked. On April 3, 1833, he played with Liszt at a concert given by the Herz brothers.[4] He appeared at a concert given by Miss Smithson. Finally, on December 15, at a concert given by Hiller at the Conservatoire, he played with Hiller and Liszt the Allegro from a Concerto for three pianos by Johann Sebastian Bach. In the spring of 1834 he went with Hiller to attend a musical festival at Aix-la-Chapelle. There he met Mendelssohn, who describes his two friends to his mother in the following terms: " He (Chopin) and Hiller have considerably improved their technical equipment. Chopin is now the first among pianists. His playing provides us with as many surprises as we find under Paganini's bow. Hiller is also a virtuoso full of strength and grace. Unfortunately they both have the Parisian mania for the tragic pose. They exaggerate the sentiment, and time and rhythm suffer for it. But since, for my part, I go to the opposite extreme, the result is that we complement each other. I seem a perfect pedant, while they are like modish young exquisites." From Aix the three musicians went on to Düsseldorf. Hiller and Chopin went up the Rhine to Coblenz. Mendelssohn accompanied them as far as Cologne.

On December 7, 1834, Chopin appeared at a concert given by Berlioz at the Conservatoire. He played an Andante, which is supposed to have been the Larghetto from the F minor Concerto. On the 25th he took part with Liszt at a concert given by Stoepel at the Pleyel Rooms. They played some Moscheles and Liszt.

On February 25, 1835, he played with the composer at Erard's Rooms a Duet for two pianos by Hiller. On March 22 he appeared at a concert at Pleyel's. On April 5 he played one of his concertos at a concert given at the Théâtre Italien in aid of the Polish refugees, with a very brilliant programme conducted by Habeneck. The *Gazette musicale* reports that he met with a great success; but this paper belonged to his publisher. It appears, on the contrary, that the audience was rather cold. Chopin was greatly applauded, on the other hand, at the *Société des concerts du Conservatoire* on April 26. The concert was given for the benefit of Habeneck, who conducted. Chopin played the Polonaise preceded by an Andante spianato (op. 22).[5] In spite of this success, he held aloof from the public for many years. "I am not fitted to give concerts," he said to Liszt: "The crowd embarrasses me, I feel stifled by their hurried breathing, paralysed by their curious glances, mute before these strange faces." And he added, with a touch of irony: "But as for you, you are intended for them by fate, for if you cannot win your public, you have the power to stun it."[6]

CHAPTER 4

DURING the brilliant years which followed his arrival in Paris, Chopin published a considerable number of works. The Polonaise for piano and violoncello, which he had composed in 1829 in Prince Radziwill's house, and afterwards revised, appeared in 1833 as op. 3. His own judgment of it is to be found in the words which he wrote on October 20, 1829: "During my visit to Prince Radziwill, I wrote an *Alla Polacca.* It is nothing but a brilliant drawing-room piece, such as ladies like." He had revised it later. On April 10, 1830, he announced that he would play it at the Lewickis' house; he had composed an Adagio as an introduction. Here we have an example of that process of agglomeration common in his bigger works. He adds: "I have already rehearsed it, and it does not sound bad." Niecks writes: "There is very little in this composition — one or two pianoforte passages and a finesse here and there excepted — that distinguishes it as Chopin's. . . . What subdued the composer's personality was no doubt the 'cello, which, however, is well provided with grateful cantilene." [1]

He was on friendly terms with Franchomme the 'cellist, and composed in collaboration with him a great Duet for piano and 'cello, based on themes from *Robert the Devil.* The opera had been produced in 1831. The piece appeared in the middle of 1833, without an opus number. Schumann is of opinion that the whole was sketched out by Chopin, and that Franchomme had nothing to do but mildly to assent. For everything that Chopin touches acquires spirit and character. Besides, Meyerbeer's themes are fine, but the finger of Chopin is apparent in the fantastic style of treating them, "veiling them here, revealing them there, in such a way that they echo in the ear and heart for a long time to come. The reproach of tediousness which nervous virtuosi perhaps bring against the piece is not without justification; at the twelfth page it is a little halting in its movements, but then at the thirteenth it plucks impatiently at the strings, in a thoroughly Chopinesque way, and from this point onwards it fleets away in wave-like figures towards the finish." [2]

Between 1832 and 1834 Chopin published the whole series of works extending from op. 6 to op. 19.[3] It includes the Mazurkas (op. 6 and 7) which his Leipzig publisher, Probst Kistner, brought out in December, 1832; the Trio for piano, violin and violoncello (op. 8, March 6, 1833); three Nocturnes (op. 9, January,

1833). These works were published by Probst Kistner alone, and a French edition did not appear till the following year. But from the summer of 1833 onwards, Schlesinger, the French publisher, bought his works, which then appeared almost simultaneously in France and Germany. There were the Twelve Grand Etudes (op. 10) announced in France in July, 1833, the German edition appearing in August; the Concerto in E minor, announced in France in July, which appeared in Germany in September, 1833. In November Breitkopf and Härtel published op. 12, Variations brillantes for the piano on Herold's *Rondeau favori* from *Ludovic;* Schlesinger did not bring out the French edition till January, 1834. This work, which is as unlike Chopin's style as can be, must have been composed in the middle of 1833, for *Ludovic,* a posthumous work, was not produced till May 16, 1833.

The year 1834 was no less prolific. Three Nocturnes (op. 15) were brought out in the month of January by Breitkopf and Schlesinger; the Rondo in E flat major (op. 16) in March by the same publishers; Four Mazurkas (op. 17) in May. The Grand Fantasia on Polish airs (op. 13) was brought out by Schlesinger in April and Probst Kistner in May. Next Schlesinger published in June, and Probst Kistner in July, the Krakowiak, Grand Concert Rondo for piano and orchestra (op. 14).

In the spring of 1834, having spent the money intended for his journey to Aix-la-Chapelle, Chopin took Pleyel the manuscript of the Waltz in E flat major; this was op. 18. It was brought out by Schlesinger at the beginning of the summer. And lastly, op. 19 was the Bolero in C major, which appeared in October, 1834.

* * *

LET us glance through these works. We already know the E minor Concerto. The Rondo in E flat major (op. 16) is fully emancipated from the classical style. It is a very light, very brilliant work in the pianistic style beloved of Chopin at the time of his second stay in Vienna.

We now come to the thirteen Mazurkas of ops. 6, 7 and 17. The mazurka is a complicated dance, in which the following evolutions were gone through: it starts by all the couples joining hands and revolving in a circle. The circle breaks up, and, led by the first couple, they all parade past the spectators. As soon as this round and procession are over, each couple dances in turn. The lady executes alternately a sliding step and a *pas de basque*. Her partner " first stamps his feet as if in challenge, then leaves his lady for a moment as if to see her better, turns round upon himself as if mad with joy and intoxicated with excitement, and soon rejoins her with passionate eagerness." [4] After an hour or two the circle is formed again, the dance ends with a round, and, frequently, the melody played by the orchestra is sung in chorus. For mazurkas have words, in which love is mingled with patriotic sorrows. "Both the music and the words," says Liszt, "reflect that opposition, which is so heroic and attractive in its effect, between the pleasure of love and the sadness caused by danger, from which arises the need of cheering one's misery." [5] The time during which one couple is dancing is a time of conversation, intrigue and love for the rest. Love-affairs are made and unmade. It was out of these little dramas that Chopin created his mazurkas. From the formal point of view the mazurka is a dance in rather slow three time, often characterised by an accent on the second beat of the bar. The first beat is itself detached or divided, giving the following rhythm:

Here is an example, taken from the Mazurka in F minor (no. 3 of op. 7):

Chopin varies this basic rhythm in a hundred different ways, and by means of this elasticity infuses reverie and poetry into the old dance. It is true that he takes as his point of departure the popular themes which he had picked up as a child from the peasants in the regions round Warsaw. But, as Liszt says, he has brought out the mysterious element of poetry in the original themes. " While preserving their rhythm, he has ennobled the melody, enlarged their compass and introduced a variety of harmonic colour as novel as the subjects to which he adapted them." He has turned dance music into a picture " of the innumerable and diverse emotions which move the heart in the course of the dance."

The first Mazurka, in F sharp minor, of op. 6 can be analysed as follows:

1. A first group of two periods, constructed upon the following figure:

This group is repeated, and so increased to four periods of eight bars each.

2. A second group in the key of the dominant, again insistently repeated, comprises a period with a fresh theme:

followed by a repetition of the first group; that is to say, a total of three periods which, when repeated, amount to six.

3. A third group begins with a period containing a third theme. This period is first repeated, and then followed by a fresh repetition of the first group, consisting of four periods. The mazurka as a whole may be compared to a song consisting of a refrain, repeated three times, with two interpolated verses. Similarly the charming Mazurka in B flat major (op. 7, no. 1) is composed, as it were, of two verses and a thrice-recurring refrain.

Such a perfectly regular form is rare. Most often, the verses and the refrain alternate capriciously.

The Mazurka in E flat minor (op. 6, no. 4) only consists of one verse between two refrains, thus assuming the normal form of a drawing-room piece, or what is known as lied form.

But what a variety of sentiments are expressed in this ordinary form! The Mazurka in F sharp minor has an easy, triumphant lilt; the one in C sharp minor is subdued and brilliant by turns, as if the couple dancing at times raised their voices for others to hear, at times let them sink to a whisper for each other alone. The one in B flat is all delicacy, tenderness and fondness. The one in F minor is an amazing mixture of whispered speeches, languishing declarations, earnest, intense reproaches, cries and murmurs and dialogues between the two voices.

This blend of sentiment, turning a few bars into a whole drama of emotion, was drawn attention to by the *Gazette musicale* of June 29, 1834 in the third mazurka of op. 17 (A flat major). " The fundamental motive of this mazurka," said the critic, " bears a stamp of deep sadness, but suddenly the poet turns gay; the most characteristic of these changes is that by which he modulates from A flat into E major. We are made conscious of this change of sentiment by the alterations of rhythm. At first Chopin only keeps up the traditional rhythm in the left hand. In the right hand, the melody which had begun so languorously [6] becomes broader and more tenuous, breaks into an adornment of triplets, lingers on the third beat, and finally ends on the first. Evidently the soul of the dancer is not in harmony with the fiddler, who emphasises the rhythm dully but strictly in the bass. And all of a sudden the dancer breaks once more into the dance. The right hand sounds a joyous melody in an animated and clear-cut rhythm, but the reverie is not entirely dissipated, and lingers on in a tendency either to place the accent on the third beat or to syncopate it. And see, the cure is not complete. Once more the tender modulations begin, and once again it falls into the dream with which it opened." It takes the ringing, sonorous modulation into E major, which struck the critic of 1834, to rouse it from its reverie.

* * *

ACCORDING to the *Gazette musicale*, the motives of the Krakowiak " are distinguished from the mazurkas, partly by their striking resemblance to the Swiss *ranz*, partly by the lightness of the rhythm in two-four time, and partly also by a particular tinge of gay animation." The critic added that the peasants in the neighbourhood of Cracow inhabit a mountainous region, and that the length of the musical phrases is due to this. Like those of the *ranz*, they have to echo far down the valleys and across the mountains. As for Chopin's Krakowiak, which is written throughout in the style of Hummel, it is quite a show piece. The piano part bristles with difficulties, fresh ones constantly occurring, until one is tempted to blame the composer for this excess of finger-work. " But to do so would be to fall into a serious error. The motives recur frequently during the whole course of the piece, whether complete or in a variety of imitations, and thanks to this wealth of artifice, together with a constant novelty of harmonic devices, they gain such wonderful variety that one cannot help repeating them from end to end with ever-renewed interest. When the art of counterpoint is united with so much poetry and such delicate taste, it is the highest resource which musical composition can offer. . . ."

The two Etudes of op. 10 were written by Chopin between his nineteenth and twenty-third year. The first mention of them by Chopin is in a letter of October 20, 1829: " I have composed a study in my own style." On November 14: " I have written several studies." They may be numbered among his finest works. Niecks points out that their distinguishing characteristics are a healthy freshness and vigour. Even those which are slow, dreamy and elegiac have none of the tenderness of the nocturnes. " He wrote them with a technical purpose," adds M. Ganche, "including in them all the harmonic effects at which he was trying to arrive on the piano, and all the pianistic difficulties." [7] And so we may find in the Etudes a compendium of Chopin's musical idiom. At the same time he concealed his pianistic science behind the magnificence of his art. The first Etude, with its spirited bass and its mighty waves of tone, has a heroic character. The second is a play of quivering light. Chopin himself told his pupil Gutmann that he never wrote a finer melody than that of the third Etude in E. One day when Gutmann was playing it, Chopin lifted his arms, clasped his hands and sighed, "O, my country!" The fourth, in spite of its sombre key (C minor) is overflowing and sparkling with life. The sixth, in E flat minor, is a plaintive nocturne. The seventh is joyous and sunlit. The eighth has a flexible and elegant grace. And into the twelfth, as we have seen, he poured all his wrath and sorrow.

The nocturne was, strictly speaking, an invention of Field's. Before that the name had been applied to serenades only, more usually for wind instruments, but sometimes for strings. Field applied it to piano pieces of a dreamy character, implying no particular form. These short, charming works did much to contribute to Chopin's popularity; he continued to publish nocturnes throughout his whole career as a composer, for the first (op. 9) date from January, 1833, and the last (op. 62) from September, 1846. In the interval between these dates he brought out some in January, 1834 (op. 15); in May, 1836 (op. 27); in December, 1837 (op. 32); in May, 1840 (op. 37); in November, 1841 (op. 48); in August, 1844 (op. 55). He usually published two at a time. But though these delicate works advanced his fame, they have made it to some extent one-sided. The elegiac, effeminate and melancholy impression which they have given of Chopin has gradually obscured his real character.

Of the three Nocturnes composing op. 9 the first, in B flat minor, is filled, says Niecks, "with voluptuous reverie and languid sweetness. It suggests twilight, the stillness of night and the thoughts to which they give rise."[8] This delicious softness is produced by the simplest and almost elementary means. The piece is constructed in lied form. The first theme is based upon the well-known figure:

This opening figure repeated with adornments forms the phrase, which is itself repeated in a slightly different guise to form the period. Thus the period appears to be composed of a single idea, floating, disintegrating and reappearing. This period in turn is repeated in full, according to a usual practice of Chopin's, for he is not at all afraid of repetitions. The last bars alone, when repeated, cast aside their languorous softness and scale the keyboard in a great outburst of passion. These two periods form the first group, or, if we so like to call it, the first theme of the lied. It is succeeded by the second, which is, as it were, murmured in a low voice in the relative major, D flat. This too is formed of a period of eight bars, based this time upon a four-bar phrase, of which the first figure is as follows:

The period is repeated note for note the first time, then a transition of four bars in A flat reintroduces the phrase of which it is composed in D flat. A fresh phrase of eight bars filled with a sentiment of sweetness and peace is then built up on the chord of the dominant seventh. It recurs like an echo and brings back the original motive in B flat minor.

But this lied form is in no way characteristic of the Nocturnes; it would even seem as if its symmetry were antipathetic to Chopin's genius, so willingly does he break away from it. The truth is that for each of these little pieces he discovers new arrangements, of inexhaustible fancy, from the simplest to the most ingenious.

If we wish to analyse the second Nocturne of op. 9, in E flat major, we must this time cut it up into phrases. It consists of eight. The second phrase repeats the first, varying the first figure very freely, but imitating the second more closely. It is as if, while copying a very regular model, the artist is suddenly seized with the spirit of adornment and imagination, sometimes at one bend of the melody, sometimes at another, and traces then and there an arabesque of incomparable grace and lightness.

The third phrase is a variation in the key of the dominant; the fourth an imitation of the first. The fifth is an imitation of the third, with the same modulation into B flat. It is as if the composer's thought hesitated and hung in suspense — *sur un bel axe d'or la tenir balancée,* (to hold it poised on a fair golden axis), as Musset was to write. The sixth phrase returns to the key of E flat and is merely an exact repetition of the fourth and first. At this point begins a long coda on an E pedal. It is adorned with gruppetti, appoggiaturas and brilliant runs.

CHAPTER 5

NICHOLAS CHOPIN had once had the three brothers Wodziński, Antony, Casimir and Felix as boarders at his school.

Frederick had become their friend and had been invited to stay with their parents at Służewo. He had played the piano with their sister, the little Maria Wodzińska. They had afterwards been parted. While Chopin was travelling to Vienna, and then to Paris, the Wodzińskis settled at Geneva. But Antony, the eldest, sometimes came to Paris, where he saw Chopin. They also corresponded. During the summer of 1834 Mme. Wodzińska invited Chopin to come to Geneva. Maria sent him a theme with variations of her own composition. Chopin replied to Felix apologising for not being able to leave Paris. He was just back from the banks of the Rhine. The theme which Mlle. Wodzińska had sent him had served him as a motive for improvisation. Finally he sent her the Valse in E flat major, the very one which had supplied him with the means for making his journey, and had just been published.

On February 28, 1835, Mme. Wodzińska asked Chopin to make a collection of autographs for her. She adds: " Are we not to have the pleasure of seeing you here? " She does not know when she will be leaving Geneva.[1]

During the summer of 1835 Chopin's father and mother went to take the waters of Carlsbad, and Frederick paid them a surprise visit there. A letter of August 16 from Nicholas Chopin to his children tells how they met: " At four o'clock we were not yet up, when someone came and knocked at our door. It was M. Zawadzki, who had come to tell us that he had been looking for us everywhere the day before with Frederick. You can well imagine that I was soon dressed, and we went off together to wake the dear child, who had learnt from my letters that I was to go to Carlsbad, and wanted to give me this most pleasant surprise; he had left all that he had to do in Paris, and spent several nights trying to get here before us. He is not changed at all, so that he appears to us just the same as when he left. You know how dearly we love him, so you can imagine how we value this mark of affection. We wept tears of joy." Frederick too enclosed a letter with his father's. " Our joy is indescribable," he writes, with that charming ardour and play of changing emotions which gives such life to his music. " We do nothing but embrace one another. Could there be a greater happiness? We go for walks, we give our arm to little Madame our mother, we talk about you, we mimic the little nephews when they are cross, we say how often we have thought of one another. We drink and eat together, we are caressing and rough to one another in turn. I am as happy as it is possible to be. These are the same habits, the same activities as those among which I grew up, this is the hand which I have not kissed for so long. Now, children, I kiss you all and beg your pardon for my scattered wits, and for not being able to talk of anything but the happiness we are feeling at present; and I who had never had anything but hope! And now it has really come to pass, this happiness, this happiness, this happiness!"[2] And so he ends on the tonic!

The Wodzińskis left Geneva. Chopin was at Carlsbad. They resolved to meet at Dresden. Frederick saw Maria again and loved her. An uncle of Maria's, a refugee living in Dresden, who was strict on the subject of the proprieties, informed her mother. But she refused to see anything in it, and put the friendship down to memories of childhood and music. The story is that on the eve of his departure the young girl offered Chopin a rose. He sat down to the piano and improvised the Waltz in F minor, which appears among the posthumous works. " One seems to hear in it," writes Count Wodziński, " first the murmur of lovers' voices, then the striking of the clock and the roll of wheels hurrying over the stony street, drowning by their clatter the sound of muffled sobs." [3]

A few days later, Chopin was back in Paris, and Maria wrote to him, though, she says, he did not like either receiving or writing letters. She draws a pretty picture of the sorrow in which he had left his friends. " On Saturday, when you left us, every one of us was walking sadly about, with eyes full of tears, in the room where, a few minutes ago, we had you among us. My father soon came in, and was sad at having been unable to say goodbye to you. My mother was in tears, and kept reminding us every moment of some characteristic ' of her fourth son Frederick,' as she says; Felix looked thoroughly depressed; Casimir tried to make his usual jokes, but that day they were not a success, for he played the clown half crying. My father made fun of us, but he himself laughed only in order not to cry. At eleven o'clock the singing-master came. The lesson went very badly; we could not sing. You were the subject of all our conversations. Felix kept asking me for the waltz (the last thing of yours which you had given us and we had heard you play). It was a pleasure to us all, for them to hear it, for me to play it, for it reminded us of the brother who had just left us." [4]

From Dresden Chopin went on to Leipzig, where Schumann and Mendelssohn were expecting him. "Sunday evening was really charming," writes Mendelssohn. "While I was playing him certain parts of my oratorio, a few good bourgeois slipped furtively into the room to see Chopin. He sat down to the piano in turn, and his new Etudes aroused general admiration; after which I again went on with my *St. Paul*. The bourgeois gaped at us; one would have thought they were listening to the conversation of a Kaffir and an Iroquois." Chopin broke his journey at Heidelberg and returned to Paris about the middle of October.

The event of the winter, for pianists at least, was Thalberg's arrival in Paris at the beginning of November. He was two years younger than Chopin, and was also a prodigy. He was a natural son of Prince Moritz von Dietrichstein and the Baroness Wetzler, and was born at Geneva on January 8, 1812. He studied in Vienna, and at the age of fifteen created a sensation there. As early as 1828 he had his first compositions published, fantasias on *Euryanthe,* on a Scottish song, on the *Siege of Corinth.* In 1830 he made his first concert tour in Germany, and wrote his Concerto, op. 5. He was in

Paris in 1835 and made his début at the house of Zimmermann, one of the most famous piano teachers then in Paris. Marmontel, who was present, has described the occasion. "That evening Mme. Viardot, Duprez and de Bériot also entered the musical lists. Thalberg had an immense success."

"The object pursued and attained by the famous virtuoso," continues Marmontel, "was to replace the old school of piano playing, in which brilliant effects were obtained by the rapidity of the diatonic or chromatic passages, by new methods covering a much wider range of keyboard, and enriching the harmonic possibilities by including effects ranging from the deepest notes of the bass to the highest extremities of the treble. ... The arrangement of the melodic phrases to suit the medium of the piano, the assignment of the most prominent notes to either hand alternately, in such a way that the strong fingers could bring out the melody more firmly, a richer harmonic structure, maintained in both hands by means of a deep bass and rapid arpeggi, such were, in brief, the devices employed by Thalberg."

The younger school of pianists at once followed in Thalberg's train in their enthusiasm for the arpeggio. Those who had already some originality and a style of their own did nothing to change it. Chopin could not bear Thalberg, and used to parody him. As for Liszt, whose royal prerogative was threatened, he hastened to the spot to challenge his rival, but too late. The duel did not take place till 1836.

Chopin, however, had returned from Germany, full of those wise resolutions which are so abundant in the hearts of true lovers. Love inspired him with a taste for retirement and a zeal for saving. " I highly approve," wrote his father on December 15 with a touch of naïveté, " your resolve to stay at home more than in previous years, but I do not advise you to go altogether into retirement. Evening parties, when they do not last too long, are a regular relaxation for you, which you require in order to give fresh life to your talent, and even to give you fresh ideas. I am equally pleased with your intention of saving something. . . ."

The letter is finished by Chopin's sister Louise. She retails to him the gossip rife in Warsaw about his passion for Maria. " When I told Mme. Linde that perhaps next year you would come to Dresden, she answered: ' Yes, if certain persons are there. Oh, Maria Wodzińska has entangled his heart.' Mme. Linde has no doubt, moreover, that the Wodzińskis angled for you. ' Mme. Wodzińska,' she said, ' monopolised him as much as she could; she always made him sit between her and Maria; this young lady, who is extremely attractive, embarrassed him. . . .' "[5]

Nicholas Chopin looked with a favourable eye upon his son's romance, and tried to make it the text of a sermon on good conduct. On January 9, 1836 he wrote to him: " I seem to notice that Dresden has become a very interesting spot to you, and appears to attract you. At your age one is not always master of oneself; one may receive impressions which are not easily effaced. But what is there to prevent you from making a little tour next spring to *riechen was du nicht gerochen hast?*[6] (savour what you have not savoured). But you will want health and funds, and you ought to think about both; it is your only means of seeing Dresden again, and anything which it may contain of interest to you, if you do not lose the impression. M. Wodziński was here before the holidays, and came to see us, but his sons were not with him. From his eagerness in asking after you, we could tell afterwards that he was aware of the report which is going round. . . ."

On February 5, 1836 Mme. Wodzińska wrote to Chopin from Dresden asking him to convey a sum of money to her eldest son, Anthony Wodziński, who lived in Paris and was rather irresponsible. " I have had the happy idea," she says, " of choosing to appeal to him who has always and everywhere given us such proofs of his friendship." She recommended her " duffer " (*nigaud*), as she calls him, to Chopin's good counsels. Chopin rejoined Maria and her mother at Marienbad in July, 1836. On August 21 they returned together to Dresden. On September 7, at nightfall, two days before his departure, Chopin asked Maria to be his wife, and requested Mme. Wodzińska's consent. He received favourable answers, but Mme. Wodzińska insisted upon secrecy. This engagement came to be alluded to among them as " the twilight." On September 14 Mme. Wodzińska writes to Chopin that she will be in Warsaw by the middle of October. " I shall see your parents and sisters," she says, " I shall tell them that you are well and in the best of spirits, but I will not mention the *twilight*. But you may be sure of my sympathy; in order fully to satisfy my hopes and test this sentiment, this precaution is necessary. Goodbye! Go to bed at eleven o'clock and drink gamboge water until January 7. . . . Take care of your health, dear Fritz. I bless you with all my soul like a loving mother." A postscript announced that Maria was sending him some slippers. " They are rather large, but she says that you ought to wear woollen stockings; such was the judgment of Paris, and I suppose you will be obedient; have you not promised? Note, at any rate, that this is a time of trial."

On the day after Chopin left Dresden, Casimir Wodziński, the gayest of the three brothers, arrived there. On the 15th he wrote to Frederick to say how he regretted not having seen him, and to give him news of Warsaw. As usual, his letter is full of jests. "Your father, whom I found not at all changed, looks as well as he did in the days when he used to scold us, make us kneel down and sometimes thrash us. I remembered the good old days when I used to come and say my lesson, and behaved like such a little imp. Indeed, as I was there on a Thursday, when everybody is gathered together, I felt as if I was still at school; I gave an account of my journey to Mme. Jendrzejewicz as if I had had a lesson to repeat; I trembled when I spoke to Barcinski, and was quite frightened when your father called me."

Evidently Casimir is not in the secret; otherwise, how can we explain his persistent allusions to the humble station in life of the Chopin family? [7] But Maria added a charming postscript: "We are inconsolable at your departure; the three days which have just gone by seemed like centuries to us; are you the same? Do you miss your friends a little? Yes, I can answer for you, and I do not think I am mistaken; at least, I require to think so. I say to myself that this 'Yes' comes from you (for you would have said it, would you not?)." She too announces that she has sent the slippers which are too big, and orders him to wear woollen stockings. And she concludes: "In a fortnight we shall start for Poland, I shall see your family: what happiness for me!" [8]

As in the previous year, Chopin had gone from Dresden to Leipzig. There he met Schumann on the 12th and gave him the work born of his love, the Ballade in G minor, which had been published in June as op. 23. "It does not seem to me to be his greatest work," writes Schumann on September 14, "but the most *genialisch* (in keeping with his genius), and I told him it was the one of his works which I liked the best. After a long silence, he said emphatically: 'I am very glad of that, for it is also the one which I prefer.'" [9]

The ballad was then a novelty. The form had been created by Loewe, and the first ones had appeared less than twenty years before in 1818. It was a piece for one voice with piano accompaniment, and was characterised by the introduction of an epic element. In treating it for the piano only, Chopin preserved this narrative character. The expression of joy or sorrow is wrapt in an atmosphere of story or legend. Finally, the instrumental ballad preserves one characteristic of the sung ballad of the Middle Ages, which had vanished since the sixteenth century: namely, the habit of refrains.

The Ballade in G minor is, in Schumann's opinion, one of the wildest and most individual compositions of Chopin.[10] It is above all, in Nieck's words, "quivering with the most intense emotions, full of sighs, sobs, groans and transports of passion. The seven introductory bars (*Lento*) begin firmly, heavily and strongly, and become progressively looser, lighter and softer, ending in a discord which certain editors have thought it their duty to correct." [11]

In the preface which Saint-Saëns has written to M. Ganche's work, he states the facts as follows: "In the last bar of the introduction," he says, "we see in the original edition a D, evidently made out of an E subsequently corrected. This supposed E gives a tone of suffering, quite in harmony with the character of the piece. Was it a misprint? Was it the composer's original intention? . . . When I questioned Liszt on the subject, the only answer I could get from him was: 'I prefer the E flat.'" [12] And Saint-Saëns concludes that he was advised to write the D by timorous and clumsy friends.[13] Niecks is also in favour of the E flat, which he calls " the emotional key of the whole poem." It is a question the sudden pain of which stabs both body and soul. Then the narrative begins, first simple and pathetic, then invaded by a growing emotion. This agitation is succeeded by the delightful second subject in E flat major, like a celestial vision. But once more passion breaks forth and carries the ballade away in that *presto con fuoco* which serves as its conclusion.

* * *

AFTER the Waltz in E flat major (op. 18), which appeared, as we have said, in June, 1834, Chopin published, in October of the same year, the Bolero in D major (op. 19). But when had he composed it? Niecks conjectures that it is a youthful work which he had turned out of a drawer. He bases this supposition upon its lack of poetry, which might indeed indicate a composition of his early years. Perhaps Chopin took the idea of a bolero from Auber, who had included one in 1828 in his *La Muette de Portici.* It is hardly necessary to say that op. 19 has no Spanish character whatever. In February, 1835, Chopin published the first Scherzo (op. 20); and in November four Mazurkas (op. 24).

What is the meaning of the Scherzo? One mystery of Chopin's work is that his music is obviously a language, but a language of which nobody knows the secret. The Scherzo opens with two sustained dissonant chords, boldly inverted, one in the four-three and the other in the six-five position. Is it a cry of despair? And does the *agitato* which follows it really represent an imprisoned soul wildly struggling to be free? This is Niecks' reading of it. Kleczyński's is different. In his view, the Scherzo in B minor answers to a period of calm after his annoyances at Vienna and the pain of his failure at Warsaw. "His ideal nature can never display any roughness; there is never too much pathos nor too much violence. . . . The principal motive, full of the mutterings of a storm, suddenly ceases, giving way to a suave and poetical melody in B major, which describes the meadows beloved of him in youth; next the melody is cut short by the two opening chords, and the storm breaks out once more, leading up to an equally bold chord,[14] and losing itself in its own tumult."[15]

The year 1836, in which his love affair took place, was much more prolific than the previous one. Chopin first revised two works composed several years before: the Concerto in F minor, and the Grand Polonaise for piano and orchestra, preceded by an Andante Spianato. These are op. 21 and 22.

The Polonaise is charmingly graceful and light. It falls into three well-defined sections. In the first, according to his habit, Chopin begins by setting out a series of themes, more or less growing out of or imitated from one another, and each forming a period, most frequently of eight bars. The two first periods are in E flat major. The third begins in F minor, then passes by the dominant of E flat minor into E flat major. The fourth is in B flat major. The tonic of B flat major next becomes the dominant of E flat major, reintroducing the opening theme in its original key.

The second section, after a preliminary period forming an introduction, gives out a fresh theme, the fifth, in A flat major.[16] A page of development, ending in C minor, leads to a sixth theme. A seventh theme in B flat major, more vigorously accentuated, reintroduces the typical polonaise rhythm, combined with developments borrowed from the first section.

Thus we arrive at the third section, which is an ornate repetition of the first, with a full and brilliant conclusion.

We have seen that the Ballade in G minor, the surviving monument of Chopin's unhappy affection for

Maria Wodzińska, appeared in June. Later on, in May, he produced two nocturnes (op. 27) and in July two polonaises (op. 29).

* * *

On October 2, 1836, Maria wrote to Chopin as follows, dating her letter from that " twilight " which was a cherished memory to them both:

" Now we are just on the point of starting for Warsaw. How happy I am at seeing all your family and, next year, *you!* Farewell till May or June at the latest."

On January 29, 1837, Countess Wodzińska thanks Chopin for having a piano sent to Służewo, and scolds him for making her a present of a magnificent volume of the *Keepsake*. Maria, as her habit was, added a postscript, but we must admit that it was rather a silly one:

" Mamma has scolded you, but I thank you prettily, very prettily, and when we meet again I will thank you even more prettily. You see that I am very lazy about writing, because putting off my thanks to our next interview dispenses me from saying much now. Mamma has described to you how we live, so nothing is left for me to tell you except that there is a thaw: great news, is it not? And above all it is most important for you to know it. The quiet life that we lead here is what I need;

that is why I love it, for the present, that is to say, for I should not want it to be so always. One makes the best of things as best one may when things cannot be otherwise than they are. I occupy myself a little to kill time. I have got Heine's 'Germany' at present, which interests me vastly. But I must close by committing you to the Divine care. I hope it is not necessary to assure you once again of the feelings of

Your faithful secretary,

Maria."

Such letters as these, empty and listless, are the despair of a lover. In 1836 Maria had lent Chopin an album. He copied into it a *Lento con gran espressione* which he had composed in 1830 for his sister Louise, besides eight melodies. The letter in which Mlle. Wodzińska thanked him was even colder and more colourless than the previous one:

"I can only write a few words to thank you for the charming book which you have sent me. I will not attempt to tell you what joy I felt on receiving it; it would be vain to do so. Pray accept my assurance of the feelings of gratitude which I owe you. Be sure of the attachment which our whole family has vowed to you for life, and especially your worst pupil and childhood's friend. Farewell! Mamma embraces you most tenderly. Thérèse (Maria's sister) keeps talking all the time of her Chopin. Farewell. Do not forget us.

Maria."

From a fiancée, such a letter is equivalent to a rupture. And indeed it foreshadowed one. This rupture took place about the middle of 1837. Maria did not resist her father's opposition to the marriage, which was due either to Chopin's low birth or to his health. Chopin was very unhappy. After his death the letters he had received from the Wodziński family were found tied up with a pink ribbon, with the inscription: *moja bieda* (my misery).[17]

In order to distract him from his sorrow Camille Pleyel and Stanislas Koźmian took him to London, where he stayed from July 11 to 22. They made him play at Broadwood, the piano-maker's, under the name of Fritz. His incognito was soon seen through. Mendelssohn wrote to Hiller on September 1: " They say that Chopin came here suddenly a fortnight ago, but he made no visits. One day he played magnificently at Broadwood's, then fled again. It seems that he is very ill."

NOTES TO PART TWO

[1] Son of the composer.

[2] Thomas Nidecki was born at Warsaw in 1800. Like Chopin, he had been a pupil of Elsner at the Conservatoire there. A State grant had enabled him to go and continue his studies at Vienna. In 1841, he was appointed conductor at the Warsaw Opera, and died there in 1852.

[3] John Matuszyński was born on December 9, 1809; he was one of Chopin's school friends and had remained one of his dearest friends. According to Karasowski (p. 122) and Scharlitt (p. 123), the letter in which Chopin describes his lodgings is addressed to Matuszyński; M. Ganche considers that it was written to his parents. Niecks adds the words "my dear ones," which are not in Karasowski. The German translation in Karasowski is a faulty one. I have followed the Polish text given by F. Hoesick (*Chopin*, I, p. 269). Scharlitt's translation (*Friedrich Chopin's Gesammelte Briefe*, Leipzig, 1911) is the more correct.

[4] Constantia Gładkowska married, in 1832, a Warsaw merchant named Joseph Grabowski and left the stage. This is the account given by Sowiński (*Słownik*, p. 124). According to Count Wodziński, she married a country nobleman. "She was an excellent wife and mother," he adds. "Alas! her soft blue eyes, which had enchanted the soul of a poet, were closed to the light. Constantia became blind. She would often sit down at the piano; she would sing her favourite tune: *Quante lagrime per te versai.* A person who knew her towards the end of her life assured me that great tears would fall, drop by drop, from her poor eyes, still limpid in spite of their blindness." *Op. cit.*, p. 130.

[5] This notice was discovered by Niecks (I, pp. 196–197). It is the only document which we have relating to Chopin's stay in Munich.

[1] Gustave Planche, *Le Salon de 1831*, Paris, Pinard, p. 15.

[2] It was no. 511 in the catalogue. The other pictures by this painter were: *Cardinal Richelieu in his chapel at the Palais Royal* (512), *An Indian armed with the Gurka kukri* (513), *Cromwell at Windsor Castle* (514), *The young Raphael meditating in his studio* (515), *Study of two tigers* (516). He also sent during the exhibition: *Guillaume de Lamarck, nicknamed the Wild Boar of the Ardennes* (this picture was exhibited as no. 2949, but is always known as *The Murder of the Bishop of Liège*); *Tam O' Shanter* (after a ballad by Burns, no. 2950); *Gulnare goes to look for Conrad in his prison, and proposes to deliver him by killing the pasha* (no. 2951, after Byron's *Corsair*); *A young girl by a well*, water-colour (2952); *Ecce Homo*, sepia (2953); See *Explication des ouvrages de peinture, sculpture, gravure, lithographie et architecture des artistes vivants exposés au Musée royal le 1er mai, 1831*, pp. 39 and 243–244.

[3] Paul Delaroche's exhibits included: *Edward V, the boy King of England, and his younger brother Richard, Duke of York* (522); *Cardinal Richelieu going up the Rhône* (523); *Cardinal Mazarin* (524), having the cards shown him when dying; the portrait of Mlle. Sontag in the part of Doña Ana, and some portraits. While the exhibition was still on, he added the picture showing Cromwell meditating before the open coffin of Charles I (2720).

[4] A. Scheffer, or the elder Scheffer, had sent his exhibits in late, and they must be looked for in the Supplements to the Catalogue. In Supplement I (nos. 2611–2619) he has an equestrian portrait of the King, Anne of Austria giving her answer to the Coadjutor, Faust, Marguerite, Christ with the children, the Return from the Army (after the ballad *Lenore*), the Tempest, and portraits of Talleyrand and Dupont de l'Eure. In Supplement I (nos. 2857–2864) there is a Henry IV, a portrait of the Duke of Orleans, a

scene from the July Days, two genre pictures suggested by Béranger's words, and some portraits.

[5] Decamps had orginally sent the *Dogs' Hospital*, *The Ass*, *Monkeys*, *Gipsy Caravan;* he replaced them by the *Turkish Patrol* and the *Turkish House.*

[6] Nos. 1800–1802 and 3087–3088.

[7] Nos. 1905–1914.

[8] Carafa was born at Naples in 1787. He was an aide-de-camp to the King, Murat, and after 1815 devoted himself to composition. He scored great successes at the Opéra-Comique, and in 1837 was received into the Institut, where he succeeded Lesueur.

[9] Great successes are marked G.S., doubtful successes S.C. (*contestés*) and failures Ch. (*chute*). *Almanach des spectacles de 1831 à 1834*, 10th year, Paris, Barba, 1834, p. 27.

[10] J. d'Ortigue, *Le Balcon de l'Opéra*, Paris, Renduel, 1833, p. 121.

[11] A. Elwart, *Histoire de la Société des Concerts du Conservatoire impérial de musique*, Paris, Castel, 1860, pp. 1–2. Fétis (*L'Europe littéraire*, July 30, 1833) asserts that for six years Cherubini refused all the petitions which were made to him in favour of reviving the concerts. It was the students of the old Conservatoire, suppressed in 1815, who had become famous artists, who joined with those of the new Royal School of Music to found the *Société des Concerts.* Many objections were still raised by the director, but he at last yielded to the inevitable.

[12] Brother of the singer. He took Tulou's place, first at the opera, and afterwards as a professor at the Conservatoire.

[13] Daniel Steibelt, born in Berlin in 1765, arrived in Paris in 1790 and became the most fashionable teacher. But he made himself unbearable and had to leave. In 1808 he finally settled in St. Petersburg. He died in 1823. Johann David Hermann had

taught Marie Antoinette the piano about 1785. As for Adam, he was the father of the composer of *Le Châlet.* He was born at Muttersholtz in Alsace in 1758, and taught the piano at the Conservatoire from 1797 to 1842. Pradher, born in 1781, was a professor at the Conservatoire from 1802 to 1829. He then retired to Toulouse, and Chopin never knew him.

[14] Zimmermann was born in Paris in 1785. He was professor of piano at the Conservatoire from 1816 to 1848. He died in 1853. Prudent, Marmontel, Ravina and A. Thomas were all his pupils.

[15] Baillot was born on October 1, 1771, and was nearing sixty. In 1834 he published his *Art du violon.* Hiller told Niecks that Chopin used to visit Baillot, who died in 1842. As for the famous Rodolphe Kreutzer, to whom Beethoven dedicated his Sonata, op. 47, Fétis speaks of him in the past, for he died in January, 1831. But Chopin may have heard his younger brother Auguste, who only died on August 31, 1832.

[16] These two letters are unknown to Niecks and are not to be found in Karasowski's collection. They form part of a lot of papers which belonged to Chopin and were bought at his death by Jane Stirling. She left them to Chopin's younger sister, Mme. Barcińska. It was believed that they had been destroyed in 1863 by the Russian soldiers, when the house inhabited by Mme. Barcińska was sacked. They survived, however, but were not published till 1902, by M. Karlowicz. There is a French translation of Karlowicz's book, by Laure Disière, *Souvenirs inédits de Frédéric Chopin,* (Paris and Leipzig, 1904) pp. 55–58.

[17] M. Karasowski, *Friedrich Chopin,* p. 148.

[18] Ferdinand von Hiller, born at Frankfort in 1811, had been in Paris since 1828. He was especially famous for his interpretation of Beethoven, having made his acquaintance in Vienna in 1827. George Alexander Osborne, composer of the famous *Pluie de*

Perles, was born at Limerick in Ireland in 1806. He has left some *Recollections of Chopin*. He was a pupil of Kalkbrenner, like Stamaty. The latter was a son of the French consul at Cività Vecchia, and was born in 1811. He had only been a pupil of Kalkbrenner since 1831. He took the place of Mendelssohn, who had been announced in the original programme, and had just arrived in Paris on his way back from Italy. As for Albert Sowiński, he was a Pole, born in 1803, who had been settled in Paris since 1830. Chopin detested him. He accused him of giving the title of *Collection of Polish songs* to a set of chansonnettes. "You know," writes Chopin, "how I have wanted, and how I have in part succeeded, in understanding our national music. So you can judge how agreeable it is to me when he catches up a motive of mine here and there, without taking into consideration how all the beauty of a song depends upon its accompaniment, and brings it out with the taste of a bar lounger or a habitué of low cabarets. And one can say nothing, for he has no understanding or feeling for anything apart from what he has taken from one."

[1] *Z życia Polaków we Francyi*, Paris, 1883, p. 115.

[2] In a letter of November 27, 1831, Elsner writes to him "Kindly be so good as to remember me to Count Plater, Grzymała and Hofmann."

[3] *L'Europe littéraire* of July 22, 1833 announces this work in the following terms: "M. Forster, a Polish refugee, is about to publish in parts a series of national songs, embracing a wide period of Polish history. The songs have been translated into verse by MM. Dumas, Soumet, etc., and have for the most part been arranged by the most distinguished composers, accompanied by illustrations by Charlet, Deveria, V. Adam, etc. The first instalment will appear in August." The title of the work was *La vieille Pologne, album historique et poétique con-*

tenant un tableau de l'histoire de ce pays, accompagné de chants ou légendes. Cf. A. Sowiński, *Słownik*, pp. 112–113.

[4] This refers to Jacques Simon Herz, born at Frankfurt in 1794, and Henri Herz, born in Vienna in 1803. They both entered the Paris Conservatoire, Jacques in 1807 and Henri in 1816, and returned as professors, Henri in 1842, Jacques as his brother's assistant in 1857. In 1833 Henri was one of the most celebrated pianists in the whole world; his brother too was a highly esteemed master.

[5] The programme was as follows: (1) Beethoven's Pastoral Symphony, (2) The Erl King, sung by Nourrit, (3) The Scherzo from the Ninth Symphony, (4) Polonaise with Introduction for Piano, composed and executed by M. Chopin, (5) Scena by Beethoven, sung by Mlle. Falcon, (6) Finale from the C minor Symphony. The aria sung by Mlle. Falcon was no doubt *Ah! perfido, spergiuro* (1810), which she had sung on March 15.

[6] F. Liszt, *F. Chopin*, p. 119.

[1] F. Niecks: *Frederick Chopin*, I, p. 201.

[2] R. Schumann, *Gesammelte Schriften*, I, pp. 203–204.

[3] Op. 4 was the Sonata in C minor left in Haslinger's hands in Vienna in 1828, but not published till after Chopin's death. At the period of Chopin's greatest success, Haslinger had had the manuscript engraved and sent the proofs to Chopin, who did not return them. This appears from a letter to his family of October 1, 1845: "The Sonata dedicated to Elsner has appeared in Vienna at Haslinger's, at least he sent me a printed proof to Paris a few years ago, but since I did not send it back to him corrected, but only told him that I should like to change many things in it, I suppose he must have stopped printing it." Indeed, the work did not appear till 1851. Op. 5 is the Rondo in the style of a Mazurka, published at Warsaw in 1827.

[4] F. Liszt, *op. cit.*, p. 65.

[5] *Ibid*, p. 60.

[6] The right hand first strikes an isolated C, then one hears the chord of the diminished seventh in A flat minor (G, B flat, D flat, F flat), acting as a triple appoggiatura. The opening C has as its sole function to soften the hardness of the attack.

[7] The first Etude in C major, on the arpeggised chords of C, G, F, etc., gives an indication of Chopin's way of playing. He wished the notes to be as legato as if they were bowed on the violin. He realised, moreover, that if worked at in a different way his object would be defeated. He said to Mme. Streicher: "Often, unfortunately, instead of teaching all this, it teaches the opposite." According to M. A. Cortot, the Etude in C major develops the strength of the fingers, and the stretch of the hand gives sureness and bravura. The second ensures the independence and evenness of the weak fingers, assures legato and gives the hand a good position, lightness, agility, etc." Chopin, 12 Etudes, op. 10, students' edition by A. Cortot (Paris, Maurice Senart). See the complete analysis of the Etudes and their editions in J. Huneker, *Chopin*, Ch. VI.

[8] F. Niecks, *op. cit.*, II, p. 262.

[1] M. Karlowicz, *Souvenirs inédits*, pp. 121–122.

[2] M. Karlowicz, *op. cit.*, p. 9.

[3] Count Wodziński, *op. cit.*, p. 250. The writer gives a facsimile of the manuscript, which is rather different from the version published by Fontana (op. 69, no. 1).

[4] M. Karlowicz, *op. cit.*, p. 122.

[5] M. Karlowicz, *op. cit.*, pp. 81–83.

[6] In the same letter Nicholas Chopin alludes to a possible travelling companion for Frederick if he returned to Dresden.

Karlowicz conjectures that he means Chopin's mother, who might go with him to ask for Maria's hand. This plan was not carried into effect (Karlowicz, *op. cit.*, p. 84).

[7] It is difficult to reconstitute their true feelings throughout this correspondence full of obscure allusions. Mme. Wodzińska seemed to be of opinion that her son Casimir's stay in Poland had had an unfortunate effect upon him. "If in Bohemia the air is saturated with opium, there it certainly is with *henbane.* What a prospect for Maria! Who knows in what state she will be in a year's time!" It looks as if Mme. Wodzińska at once foresaw the difficulties and perhaps the change in her daughter. She herself, on the 14th, a week after the engagement, defends herself against the suspicion of wishing to take back her consent. In spite of her protestations, it looks as if she had hardly believed in this marriage.

[8] These letters are in Karlowski's collection, pp. 127–129. We see from them that Chopin left Dresden on the last Saturday before September 14, i.e., the 9th. The betrothal, according to Count Wodziński, took place the day before. But he places the scene of it at Marienbad in the month of August.

[9] This letter is quoted by Karasowski, p. 177, and is addressed to Dorn, Schumann's master, at Riga. It runs as follows: "Von Chopin habe ich eine neue Ballade (I have a new ballade from Chopin)." It seems indeed as if it was a copy he had sent, and not a first draft. Moreover, the word *neue* has led people to suppose that it was the second ballade in F major, which did not appear till 1840, and is actually dedicated to Schumann. The dedication was not added until 1839, on his return from Majorca, and Chopin was not sure whether to put his friend's name on the Preludes or the Ballade. It is certain, however, that as early as 1836 a first version was sketched out, and that Chopin played it to Schumann, for the latter alludes to this in an article in 1841.

The conclusion had then been in F major; in the published version it was in A minor (*Gesammelte Schriften*, III, pp. 64–65).

[10] *Eine seiner wildesten eigentumlichsten Kompositionen* (*op. cit.*, III, p. 64).

[11] F. Niecks, *op. cit.*, II, 268.

[12] Ed. Ganche, *op. cit.*, p. 10.

[13] The correction to D ends the introduction on the second inversion of the chord of the tonic. This is the reading adopted by Reinecke in his collected edition.

[14] It is the chord F sharp, B, D, E sharp, G, i.e., a chord of the seventh on a dominant pedal.

[15] J. Kleczyński, *Frederic Chopin*, p. 12.

[16] This theme forms the subject, as usual, of a period of eight bars, in which it is heard twice; but the second time, it is in G major. This modulation into a key a semitone lower produces a charming effect.

[17] In 1841 Maria Wodzińska married Count Joseph Skarbek, but was not happy with him. She was separated from him in 1848. The marriage was annulled at Rome. She next married M. Orpiszewski, whom she kept alive for eighteen years. He died in 1881. She had a son whom she lost at the age of four. She was still alive in 1886 when Count Wodziński published his book, which is, however, full of fanciful episodes and mistakes. She died in 1896. Cf. F. Hoesick. *Chopin*, II, p. 225

PART THREE

LÉLIA

1838-1847

CHAPTER 1

In 1835 Liszt went to Geneva to join the beautiful Comtesse d'Agoult, who had left her husband and daughter for his sake. She was twenty-nine years old. Now Liszt knew Alfred de Musset, and through Musset, at the end of 1834, he had made the acquaintance of George Sand. The Comtesse d'Agoult admired the novelist. Liszt brought the two women together. George Sand came to Geneva in 1836. In the autumn the Comtesse d'Agoult and Liszt came in turn to Paris. They settled at the Hotel de France in the Rue Laffitte. George Sand came to stay there with them. Liszt spoke to her of Chopin.[1] She wished to know the musician, the poet of those impalpable landscapes which she had herself described and dreamed over in her *Lettres d'un voyageur*.

Chopin had been on friendly terms with Liszt since his arrival in Paris. The portrait of the Hungarian musician was the only one adorning the Polish musician's sitting-room. One evening Liszt and a few friends paid a surprise visit to Chopin's rooms. Liszt has left a brilliant description of this evening, in which it is difficult to distinguish memory from invention.[2] He describes the room lit only by a few candles round a Pleyel piano; the ghostly furniture in white covers, appearing to listen to the music; a sheet of light spreading from the piano over the floor, stretching towards the hearth, on which gleamed fitfully the orange flames; Heine, Meyerbeer, Nourrit and Hiller gathered in this zone of light, Eugène Delacroix remaining amazed and absorbed. The old Niemcewicz listened with gloomy gravity while his *Chants historiques* came to life under the musician's fingers. Apart from all the rest could be seen the unbending profile of Mickiewicz. A mirror reflected the Comtesse d'Agoult's blonde curls. " Sunk in an armchair, with her elbows on a console, was Madame Sand, curiously attentive and graciously subjugated."

This must have happened at the end of 1836. George Sand and Chopin met again in the improvised salon over which the Comtesse d'Agoult gracefully presided at the Hôtel de France. " It was at her lodging, or through her," says George Sand, " that I made the acquaintance of Eugène Sue, the Baron Ekstein and Chopin." But the novelist had produced the most unfortunate impression upon the musician. Hiller writes to

Liszt: " One evening you gathered together at your lodging the élite of French literature. George Sand certainly cannot have been missing. On our way home Chopin said to me: ' How repellent that woman Sand is! Is she really a woman? I could almost doubt it. . . .' "

In January, 1837, George went to Nohant, where she spent the whole year. Chopin was invited to come and see her, but did not come. As we have seen, he was still mourning over his broken engagement. We saw how he was in London in July; it is possible that he was at Ems in September. We lose sight of him until February, 1838, when he was again in London and played before the Court.

In a letter of March 2, 1838, Balzac describes to Mme. Hanska a visit which he had just made to Nohant: " I came to rest at the château of Nohant the Saturday before Lent, about half-past seven in the evening, and found our friend George Sand in her dressing-gown, smoking a cigar after dinner at the fireside in a great lonely room. She had on pretty yellow slippers trimmed with fringe, smart stockings and red trousers. So much for the moral side. As for the physical, she has got a chin as double as a canon's. She has not got a single grey hair, in spite of her terrible troubles; her swarthy complexion has not changed; her fine eyes are just as brilliant; she looks just as stupid when she is thinking, for, as I told her after studying her, the whole character of her face lies in the eye. She has been at Nohant for a year, very depressed and working enormously. . . . She goes to bed at six in the morning and gets up at midday." They talked about Jules Sandeau, who had disappointed them both. "However, she was even more unhappy with Musset, and here she is, in deep retirement, condemning both marriage and love, because she met with nothing but disappointments in both conditions."

The pitiless Balzac did not foretell a favourable future. "She is not lovable," he wrote, "and consequently she will only be loved with great difficulty. She is a bachelor, an artist, she is great, generous, devoted, chaste; she has a man's features: ergo, she is not a woman." And later: "In fine, she is a man, and all the more so since she wishes to be one, since she has gone outside the position of a woman, and is not a woman. Women attract; she repels, and as I am very much of a man, if she produces that effect upon me, she must produce it upon men like me; she will always be unhappy. And so she now loves a man who is inferior to her,[3] and in such an arrangement there can be only disenchantment and disappointment for a woman with a beautiful soul. . . ."

She was thirty-four years of age; Chopin was twenty-eight. On the very day when Balzac wrote the letter which we have just read, Chopin was playing at a concert given by the pianist Valentin Alkan, who was three years younger than himself, and had arranged Beethoven's Symphony in A major for eight hands and two pianos. The parts were taken by Alkan, Chopin, Zimmermann, who had been Alkan's master, and Gutmann, a young pupil of Chopin's.[4]

A few days later Chopin went to Rouen to give a concert for the benefit of his fellow-countryman Professor Orłowski. " It was quite an event," writes Legouvé in the *Gazette musicale* of March 25. " It was only necessary that there should be a good action to perform, in memory of his country too, for him to surmount his reluctance to play in public. Well, his success was immense! immense! All these exquisite melodies, these unspeakable refinements of execution, this melancholy and passionate inspiration, all that poetry of execution and of composition which grips both the heart and the imagination at the same time, affected, moved and intoxicated his five hundred auditors . . . ; at every moment the hall was swept by those electrical thrills, those murmurs of ecstasy and amazement which are the applause of the soul. Come now, Chopin! Come! Let this triumph decide you; cease to be selfish, give us all more of your fine talent: consent to be taken for what you are, put an end to the great controversy which divides artists, and when people ask who is the first pianist in Europe, Liszt or Thalberg, let everybody be in a position to answer, with those who have heard you: It is Chopin."

About the same time, Heine wrote in the Stuttgart *Dramatic Review:* "Poland has given him her chivalrous sentiment and historic sorrows; France, her easy elegance and grace; Germany, her dreamy profundity . . . ; but nature gave him a tall, slender, elegant, if rather sickly figure, the noblest of characters, and genius. We must certainly grant that Chopin has genius in the full acceptance of the word. He is not only a virtuoso but a poet as well; he is able to reveal to us the poetry which dwells in his soul; he is a poet-musician, and there is nothing to compare to the enjoyment he affords us when he improvises upon the piano. He is, then, neither a Pole, a Frenchman nor a German; he reveals a higher origin; he comes from the land of Mozart, Raphael and Goethe; his true country is the land of poetry."

CHAPTER 2

DURING George Sand's visits to Paris in the spring of 1838 for the lawsuit in which she was engaged with her husband, she met Chopin, who was thoroughly upset by the breaking off of his engagement. The reserve which Chopin had shown towards her soon changed into friendship, and even this friendship soon underwent a change.

How did this sympathy arise? Nothing is known on the subject. M. Wladimir Karenine, in his book on George Sand, confines himself to recalling the grief which the Wodzińskis had inflicted upon Chopin, and concludes: "When the sympathy of a great soul, free, ardent and ready to love, came to him, it must at once have flooded with light, ardour and inextinguishable passion this heart which had never yet met with real love nor with a heart its own equal." [1]

As a matter of fact we do not know anything about the beginnings of this love. The first document to make any allusion to it is a very enigmatic letter which George Sand wrote from Nohant to Mme. Marliani, on May 28, 1838.[2]

"*Ma chère belle,* I have received your kind letters,

and I hesitate to answer you exhaustively, for you know that the weather is variable during the season of love.

"One may say many 'yeses,' 'noes' and 'buts' in a week, and one often says 'This is unbearable' in the morning, only to say in the evening, 'This really is supreme happiness.'

"So I am waiting to write to you properly till my barometer records something, if not stable, at any rate sure for a certain time. I have not the slightest little reproach to make, but that is not a reason for being happy."

The cause of this uncertainty was perhaps that George Sand had heard of the engagement with Maria Wodzińska. She did not know — and this was strange — that the engagement had been broken off. And for her part, she had been for nearly a year the mistress of Mallefille, whose happiness was sacred to her. In this difficulty she consulted Albert Grzymała, a friend of Chopin's. The consultation seems to have been a delicate matter. George Sand closed it by a very long and very curious letter which M. Karenine has published.[3] She does not want to take Chopin away from Maria Wodzińska: "I do not want to play the part of a bad angel. I am not Meyerbeer's *Bertrand,* and I shall not struggle against the friend of his childhood if she is a good and pure Alice; if I had known that there was a tie in our child's life, a sentiment in possession of his soul, I should never have bent over a perfume reserved for another altar. In the same way he would no doubt have avoided my first kiss if he had known that I was, as it were, married. We did not deceive each other, we yielded as it were to a passing wind, which carried us both away to other regions for a few moments."

But they had to come back to earth. She therefore asks Grzymała whether Maria seems more likely to make Chopin happy than she does herself. "I ask to be told which of us two he must forget or abandon for his own repose and happiness, for his life, in fact, which seems to me too precarious and frail to stand great suffering. If he came and placed his existence in my hands, I should be very much alarmed, for, having accepted another, I could not take the place to him of what he would have left for me."

So God would not allow them to perform their earthly pilgrimage side by side. They were to meet in heaven: for so George Sand calls the sublime regions to which Chopin and love were able to lead her; a little while back she had spoken of celestial embraces and voyaging through the empyrean. "The fleeting moments which we spend there will be so beautiful that they will be worth a whole life spent here below."

She will renounce even these celestial embraces if Maria is really going to give Chopin a pure, true happiness. "If his soul, excessively and perhaps madly scrupulous, can also have wise scruples, and refuse to love two different creatures in two different ways, if the week that I shall spend with him in one season is to prevent him from being happy in his home for the rest of the year; then, yes then, I swear to you that I shall study to make him forget me." But if Chopin is less scrupulous, or less happy, "if his domestic happiness can and must be compatible with a few hours of chaste passion and sweet poetry" — or if this domestic happiness does not exist — then, instead of shunning him whom she loves, George dreams of drawing as near to him as possible (without compromising Mallefille's peace of mind, she says), of recalling herself gently to his memory during his hours of rest and beatitude, of occasionally clasping him chastely in her arms, "when the celestial wind is pleased to carry us away and bear us through the air."

But above all, if the marriage with Maria is to be the grave of this artist's soul, ah, then it must be prevented; even Chopin's religious scruples must be overcome. If this fiancée is to be a gaoler, as Russia is of Poland, George prays Heaven for all the seductions of Armida in order to keep the poor child. Even if he has seduced her, and is marrying her as in honour bound, he should not be too much governed by his scruples. One does not owe the future as payment for the past, for the past is limited and the future is infinite. The best thing would be if Chopin's heart, like that of George Sand, could contain two loves, one of which would be the body and the other the soul.

" As to the question of possession or non-possession," she added, " that seems to me a question of secondary importance to the one with which we are now concerned." She admits that she has no definite ideas on the subject. If they are to live together, complete union is best; if they are to live apart, it is a matter of prudence and true virtue to abstain. But even this restraint ought to be a sacrifice. She had been very shocked when, at the moment of leaving her, Chopin appeared to despise the very thing which she refused him. " He seemed to disdain human grossness as the pious do, to blush for the temptations he had undergone, and to dread defiling our love by another ecstasy. This way of looking at the supreme embrace of love has always been repugnant to me. . . ."

All these deliberations led to the usual result. But we know nothing about the early months of the connection. As for the works published during this period: from July, 1836, to October, 1837, during the fifteen months corresponding to the engagement and the rupture with Maria Wodzińska, Chopin had published absolutely nothing.[4] In October, 1837, he produced the twelve Etudes of op. 25, dedicated to the Comtesse d'Agoult. Even these Etudes, according to Chopin's testimony, were almost all composed at the same time as those of op. 10, that is to say, before the summer of 1833. They are just those which he had left. Only a few of them, of masterly composition, must have been composed later. Such are the first, in A flat, (according to an interpretation attributed to Chopin, a little shepherd, sheltered in a grotto during a storm, plays a peaceful melody on the flute), and the magnificent twelfth in C minor. In December he published the Impromptu (op. 29), four Mazurkas (op. 30), the Scherzo in B flat minor (op. 31), and two Nocturnes (op. 32).

The Scherzo, inspired by the rupture with Maria, bears in its questionings, its reproaches, its caressing phrases, the obvious signs of a love full of suffering and doubt. Schumann is quite right about it. He compares it with a poem of Byron's, "so tender, so audacious, as full of love as of mockery." Niecks in his turn points to the veil of melancholy clouding those phrases which ought to be the most joyful. He remarks upon the "capricious, impulsively passionate first section" in B flat minor and D flat minor, the tender melancholy of the *con anima* which follows it; next, after the repetition which completes the cycle of this first section, the entry of a phrase in A, more mysterious than the Gioconda's smile; finally, the passage in C sharp minor, more urgent and clearly-defined, like an awakening from the preceding dream. "I venture to say," he adds, "that this scherzo is a very important composition, richer and more varied in emotional incidents than the other works of Chopin which bear the same name."[5]

It was at this time that Chopin started his habit of only publishing works at the end of the year. Thus in 1838 it was not till November that he produced the four Mazurkas (op. 33), and in December the three Valses (op. 34). He must have sent the manuscripts to the publisher during the summer, perhaps when he was making his plans for departure, and in order to provide for the expenses of the journey.

He did the same with the Preludes (op. 28). He sold them to Camille Pleyel, to whom they are dedicated, before leaving Paris. But they were as yet only sketched out. Pleyel gave 2,000 francs for them, 500 of which were paid down to Chopin, the rest to be paid as the manuscripts were delivered to him. The Preludes actually appeared nearly a year later, in September, 1839. They are the surviving witness to the early days of love between Chopin and George Sand.

CHAPTER 3

MAURICE, George Sand's son, was a delicate child, for whom the doctors had prescribed wintering in a warm climate. George Sand had planned to spend the winter of 1838–1839 in Italy, but afterwards, on the advice of her friends the Marlianis, she decided to visit Majorca.

"While I was making my plans and preparations for departure," she writes in her *Histoire de ma vie*, "Chopin, whom I saw every day, and whose genius and character I dearly loved, said to me, over and over again, that if he was in Maurice's place, he would soon be cured himself. I believed him, but I made a mistake: I did not include him in the journey instead of Maurice, but together with Maurice. His friends had been pressing him for a long time to go and spend some time in the South of Europe. He was believed to be consumptive. Gaubert examined him and vowed to me that he was not. 'You will indeed save him,' he said to me, 'if you give him air, exercise and rest.'" [1]

When, many years later, she wrote *L'histoire de ma vie*, George Sand represented things as follows: Chopin asked to be taken with them; she hesitated, weighed all reasons with superior prudence, and made this love-sick child, whom she describes as raving mad, listen to reason. " However, I begged Chopin to weigh his moral strength well, for for many years past he had never contemplated without alarm the prospect of leaving Paris, his doctor, his friends, even his lodging and his piano. He was the slave of habit, and any change, however small, was a terrible event in his life."

Was this the way things really happened? All this wisdom hardly squares with the bold calculations of the letter to Grzymala. So early as that, George Sand was looking forward to voyages in the ether, wherever the celestial wind should bear them away. And in *Un hiver au midi de l'Europe,* which appeared in 1841 in the *Revue des Deux Mondes,* she writes: " All of us, happy or unhappy, idlers and newly-married couples, lovers and hypochondriacs, dream of some poetic refuge, we all depart to find some retreat in which to love, or some shelter in which to die." It is natural to see in these lines the true reason for their departure. When winter came they would have been separated, Chopin in Paris and George Sand at Nohant. Love once again induced them to wander.

George Sand started first, travelled slowly, visited

friends; by way of Lyons and the Rhône she arrived at Perpignan on October 29 or 30. Chopin left Paris mysteriously. Only a few very intimate friends knew the destination of his journey. Fontana sent him his correspondence, and undertook to forward the answers. Chopin arrived at Perpignan at the beginning of November. Two hours before the departure of the boat, George Sand wrote to Mme. Marliani: " Chopin arrived at Perpignan yesterday, as fresh as a rose, and as rosy as a turnip: in good health too, having borne his four nights in the coach heroically."

The *Phénicien* transported them from Perpignan to Barcelona, *El Mallorquín* from Barcelona to Majorca. The crossing took place by night, as it still does. The night was warm and dark. The sea was phosphorescent. All things slept. The man at the steering-wheel was singing. Chopin listened to this chant which had come long since from the East, and was so similar to the Slav melodies. George Sand has described their mingled impressions, or rather Chopin's, as noted by her. " Everybody on board was asleep, except the steersman, who in order to struggle against the danger of doing likewise, sang all night, but in such a soft, restrained voice that one would have thought he was afraid of waking the men of the watch, or else that he was half asleep himself. We never tired of listening to him, for his song was of the strangest character. He followed a rhythm and modulations quite foreign to our usages, and seemed to let his voice wander at its own sweet will, like the smoke of the vessel, carried away and wafted on the breeze. It was a reverie rather than a song, a sort of listless meandering of the voice, in which thought had but little part, but which followed the rocking of the ship and the gentle surge of the waves, resembling a vague improvisation, yet imprisoned in a form both soft and monotonous."

At Palma there were neither hotels nor apartments. Finally a certain Señor Gomez let them a country villa called in Catalan *Son Vent,* the House of the Wind, for fifty francs a month.

In 1836 Mendizabal had confiscated the property of the religious orders, and the Charterhouse of Valdemosa, three leagues from Palma, had been shut up. Chopin and George Sand rented for thirty-five francs a year one of the dwellings intended for the Fathers. According to the rule of the order, it was composed of three cells, the middle one destined for prayers, the one on the right serving as a bedroom, the one on the left as a workroom and refectory. The whole opened upon the monks' garden, with pomegrantes, lemon trees, orange trees, brick-paved walks and fragrant arbours, a regular bower of flowers and verdure. This garden on the slope of a mountain, hanging like a balcony over the valley, was upheld by a terrace, below which descended tiers of orange-trees, then lower down vines, and lower still almond-trees and palm-trees; and as a background to the picture, the blue line of the sea. In the middle of November, George Sand and Chopin settled at Son Vent. Their friends, who were shaky in geography, had sent them to the Mediterranean in the middle of the rainy season. During the first few days, the weather was splendid; but one night the first deluge descended. Señor Gomez' house became uninhabitable. " The walls were so thin," writes George Sand, " that the whitewash with which our rooms were plastered swelled up like a sponge. For my part I have never suffered so badly from the cold, though it was not really very cold, but for us, who are used to heating our houses in winter, this house without a fireplace enfolded us like a cloak of ice, and I felt paralysed." At the beginning of their visit, while it was still fine, they had made a splendid, but very tiring excursion to the northern coast, no doubt in the direction of the present site of the Archduke Salvador's villa. Chopin, who had travelled three leagues over difficult country, returned exhausted and fell ill. The bad weather made him worse. " We could not get used to the suffocating fumes of brasiers," writes George Sand, " and our invalid began to suffer and to cough. From this time onward we became an object of horror and alarm to the natives." The Majorcans were afraid of infection. Gomez urged the travellers to leave his house, after paying for replastering it and renewing the whitewash, and buying all the household linen which they had used and infected. There remained Valdemosa. They moved in on December 15, on a cool, sunny day.

They had tables, wicker chairs, a white wood sofa furnished with cushions of mattress-ticking stuffed with wool, and a beautiful great oak Gothic pulpit with carved pinnacles and ornaments, which the sacristan had fetched from the chapel, and the body of which served as a bookcase. Their brown leather trunks looked like luxurious furniture. The alcove, containing a bed, had a travelling rug hung across it. The stove was adorned with a pot of Felanitz ware. The floor was covered with plaited straw mats and sheepskins. For more than a month Chopin had nothing to play on but a Majorcan piano. At last, in the middle of January, the piano sent by Pleyel arrived, though they had been advised of its arrival at Marseilles on December 1.[2]

There was nobody in the Charterhouse but the sacristan, the chemist, and a certain Maria Antonia, who placed herself at the service of the travellers, and was obliging, pious and predatory. She was helped by two native servant-girls, La Nina and La Catalina, who were as great thieves as herself.

The bad weather had cut off communications with Palma, so food supplies became very difficult. The only meat to be had was pork, which Chopin could not bear, or old hens. The bread arrived from Palma soaked with rain. The dirty servants seasoned the food with pepper, tomatoes and garlic. All that was good were the fruit and wine. " We had to live chiefly on fruit," writes George Sand in *Un Hiver à Majorque*, " washed down with excellent spring water or wine of a muscat flavour; besides bread, vegetables and sometimes a little fish or lean meat roasted without any butter." The difficulties were increased by the quarantine in which the travellers were kept. The peasants, not seeing them come to church, called them pagans and Mahometans, refused to have any dealings with them, or quadrupled their prices; at the first protest, they put their wares back into their baskets and walked off in a dignified way.

These gloomily romantic surroundings delighted

George Sand. " I was not sorry," she says, " to see once and for all, thoroughly and in reality, what I had only seen in dreams or in fashionable ballads, or in the convent scene in *Robert the Devil* at the opera." Even she shuddered at such an impressive sight. " I must own," she says, " that I never went through the cloister in the evening without a certain emotion of mingled anguish and pleasure, which I should not have liked to show before my children for fear of communicating it to them." Moreover, she made use of these surroundings and emotions in writing fantastic stories like *Spiridion.*

But while she was drawing upon Valdemosa for this questionable literature, poor Chopin, nervous and ill as he was, was receiving impressions of terror. " He became utterly demoralised. He could bear pain with a fair amount of courage, but he could not control his uneasy imagination. Even when he was well, the cloister was filled for him with terror and phantoms. He did not say so, and one had to divine it. On returning from my nocturnal explorations with the children, I would find him at ten o'clock at night sitting at the piano, pale and with haggard eyes, and his hair almost standing on end. It took him some moments to recognise us."

A passage follows which is very valuable for understanding the Preludes: "Then he would make an effort to laugh, and play us sublime things which he had just composed, or rather, terrible and heartrending ideas which had just taken possession of him, as it were without his knowledge, during this time of solitude, melancholy and alarm. It was here that he published the finest of those short pages which he modestly called preludes. They are masterpieces. Many of them call up to the mind's eye visions of dead monks and the sound of their funeral chants, which obsessed him; others are suave and melancholy; these would come to him in his hours of sunshine and health, amid the sound of children's laughter beneath his window, the distant thrum of the guitar, and the song of the birds among the damp leafage; or at the sight of pale little roses blooming above the snow. Others again are dreary and sad, and wring the heart while charming the ear." And she relates how one day, on returning with Maurice from Palma through torrents of rain, she found Chopin weeping, as he played a fine prelude which he had just composed. He rose with a loud cry, and said with a distracted look: "Ah, I was sure that you were dead!" He had been waiting for them in an agony of anxiety; then, as he grew calmer, almost falling into a trance as he played, he had dreamt that he himself was dead. He was drowned in a lake; icy drops of water were falling heavily upon his breast. It was the rain falling upon the roof which had suggested this nightmare vision to him. People have tried to find which prelude this was. Wodziński opts for Prelude no. 6 in B minor. It is a simply constructed page, the main subject of which is the following figure, with the melody in the left hand.

This figure is repeated a certain number of times in free sequence. It was this rudimentary development of the Prelude which later disconcerted Schumann. " I must confess," he says, " that I had imagined them to be different, and treated, like his Etudes, in the grandest style. Almost the opposite is the case: they are sketches, beginnings of studies, or, if you prefer, ruins, a few feathers dropped by an eagle." But he at once modifies this harsh judgment. " Yet in every piece," he adds, " there is the same speaking style — which *is* Frederick Chopin; he can be recognised even in his silences, which are instinct with passion. He is and remains the proudest and most audacious poetic genius of his time."

The reason which might induce us to see in the 6th Prelude the one described by George Sand is the persistence in the soprano part throughout the whole piece of a quaver falling like a drop of water.

Liszt was of a different opinion. " A terrible storm broke out," he says. " Chopin knew that his beloved companion was in the neighbourhood of the swollen torrents, and had a violent attack of nerves. Nevertheless the electricity with which the air was surcharged at last passed over, and the crisis was at an end. He returned to his piano and improvised the splendid *Fis moll.*" This was the eighth Prelude in F sharp minor.[3] M. Ganche opts for no. 15 in D flat major. But M. Karenine thinks that this prelude 15 is the one which evokes the funeral procession of the monks. No. 17, on the contrary, is in his opinion full of sunshine, the song of birds and the scent of the pale little roses.

The manuscript of the Preludes was sent to Fontana at the beginning of January. We may remember that Pleyel was then to have paid him 1,500 francs, the balance of the 2,000.[4] The German edition was sold to Probst.

How can we bend unmoved over this short collection, which is the sole revelation left us by Chopin of this year of passion and suffering, of this first year of a love which lasted ten years?

The first Prelude is of extreme simplicity. There is a first period of eight bars in C major. This first period is merely a sequence of quite simple chords, but so broken up that they may be interpreted as appoggiaturas, ornaments and effects of suspense.

It is followed by two periods of eight bars. After an impassioned working-up Chopin writes *calmato,* and does indeed conclude with a peaceful fourth period serving as a coda and based up to the end on a pedal C.

The second Prelude in A minor is, if possible, even simpler. It starts in E minor. The phrase on which it is based is heard in different keys, and it is not till the third repetition that it occurs in A minor. And that is the end. The accompaniment, which is first heard by itself, is the chord of E, the B being varied with A sharp. This variation, sounded together with the mediant G, forms a diminished seventh which gives its colour to the whole prelude.

The third Prelude, in G major, is delicious, but it is made out of nothing, for the charming line of the accompaniment and the suave cantabile of the first phrase are simply the chord of the tonic. A second phrase in D is in its turn no more than a progression from the chord of the dominant seventh to the dominant seventh of G. The first period is repeated in the second, in accordance with a very familiar device of Chopin's, which consists in repeating the first phrase of the period unchanged, and modifying the second, as if a fresh dream had taken possession of him. This time the second phrase is in C, then it returns in G, and is prolonged so as to extend over nine bars. And that is all. The last six bars are a delicate arpeggio on the chord of the tonic.

The fourth, in E minor, is made up of two periods of twelve bars,[5] and based on the interval of a second, major or minor, which is heard incessantly in the soprano part in a melancholy falling movement, while in the other voices batteries of quavers move, also by step, in strictly graduated chromatics. The ninth Prelude is nothing but a phrase of four bars, stated three times, the first time in E major, the two other times in a modulation: imagine a branch of flowers, first motionless, then twice stirred by the breeze. The twelfth, in G sharp minor, begins with a simple alternation of the chords of the tonic and dominant, on which is imposed in the soprano a rising chromatic passage instinct with tempestuous emotion.

Chopin next composed and sent in a second parcel to the same friend the second Ballade and two Polonaises. He asked Pleyel for 1,000 francs for the Ballade, the German rights being sold to Probst for 500 francs; [6] as for the two Polonaises, he offered Pleyel the rights for France, England and Germany, and asked him for 500 francs for them. So that the three pieces ought to have brought him in three thousand francs in all.

The negotiations entrusted to Fontana were very arduous, and were still going on long after Chopin's return to France. Pleyel considered the manuscripts too dear. Chopin was exasperated, and wrote to Fontana to offer them to Schlesinger at a lower price, 800 francs for the Ballade and 1,000 to 1,200 francs for the Polonaises. Next he changed his mind: "As for the Ballades and Polonaises, do not sell them either to Schlesinger or Probst. . . . If you have given the Ballade to Probst, take it back, even if he were to offer you a thousand francs. You can tell him that I have asked you to keep it till my return, and that then we shall see." Then he decided to keep back the English rights, and empowered Fontana to treat with Wessel of London for six manuscripts at 300 francs each. In the end the Ballade appeared in September, 1840, and the Polonaises in November, the German edition being published by Breitkopf and the French edition by Troupenas.

* * *

But Chopin's health was growing worse and worse. Both physically and morally he was at the end of his tether. "His spirit was flayed alive," says George Sand, "a crumpled roseleaf, a fly's shadow made him bleed. Except for me and the children, everything beneath the Spanish sky was hateful and revolting to him. He was dying of impatience to be gone, even more than of the discomforts of our accommodation." [7] As soon as the first fine days arrived, they resolved to return to France. The journey from Valdemosa to the sea was terrible. The night on *El Mallorquín*, spent among the grunting of a hundred or so pigs and the oaths of the captain, was even worse. The captain had given Chopin the worst bed, saying that it would have to be burnt. At Barcelona he was spitting blood by the basinful. George Sand sent a note to the commandant of the

French ship *Méléagre* which was stationed there. He took the travellers on board, and the doctor on the *Méléagre* managed to stop the haemorrhage. On February 15, 1839 George Sand wrote to Mme. Marliani: " Here I am at Barcelona. Heaven send that I get away soon and never more set foot in Spain! " When Chopin was a little better, the French consul's carriage drove him to the hotel. The travellers stayed there a week, then sailed once more in the *Phénicien*. On February 26, George Sand wrote from Marseilles to Mme. Marliani: " At last, dear, here I am back in France! A month longer, and Chopin and I should have died in Spain: he of melancholy and disgust, I of rage and indignation."

CHAPTER 4

At Marseilles the travellers stayed at the Hôtel de Beauvau. George Sand had a long-standing acquaintance with Dr. Cauvières. He found Chopin's health seriously impaired; but seeing that he was recovering strength quickly, he promised a cure, and assured them that by taking great care he might live for a long time. In any case, he advised him to prolong his stay in the south, and forbade him to return to Paris before the summer.

The commercial bustle of the place was not very pleasing to the travellers: "I have only to put my nose out of the window looking over the street or the harbour," writes George Sand, "to feel myself turning into a sugar-loaf, a soap-box or a packet of candles. Fortunately Chopin and his piano while away the tedium and bring back poetry into the house." During that month of March the mistral blew at times, and they had to surround themselves with screens in the middle of their rooms. Tiresome callers were another drawback. "There is a mob at my door," writes George Sand somewhat severely, "all the literary riff-raff are persecuting me and all the musical riff-raff are after Chopin."

Chopin was much better. He slept like a child, which gave the doctor great hopes. One evening, while he was asleep, George wrote Mme. Marliani a charming letter full of love and pity. " For a few days past he has been overcome with sleep, which I think a very good thing, but against which his restless, active spirit rebels. It is no use, he must sleep all night and a good part of the day. . . . Chopin is an angel, his goodness, tenderness and patience sometimes make me anxious; I imagine that his organisation is too delicate, too exquisite and too perfect to live our gross, heavy, earthly life for long. At Majorca, when he was sick unto death, he made music which had the very fragrance of Paradise, but I am so used to seeing him in heaven that I do not feel that life or death prove anything for him. He himself is hardly aware in what planet he exists; he makes no account of life as we conceive it and as we feel it." [1] In April he accompanied George Sand on an excursion to Genoa. On April 24, when the coffin of Adolphe Nourrit was brought back from Naples, where the singer had been killed — perhaps by his own act — by falling out of a window, Chopin played the organ at the service, which took place, in spite of the bishop's protests, at Notre-Dame-du-Mont. A crowd thronged to attend it, and chairs were hired for fifty centimes, which was a great deal. But the public was disappointed. Chopin played Schubert's *Die Gestirne* on a bad organ, of which he had chosen those stops which were the least shrill, " not," writes George Sand, " in an exalted and glorious tone, as Nourrit used to do, but in a gentle, plaintive tone like an echo from another world."

On the morning of May 22, 1839, the travellers left Marseilles. George Sand's carriage was waiting for them at Arles. They came back " quite quietly, sleeping at the inns like good bourgeois." By the end of the month they were settled at Nohant. On June 25 George Sand writes to Mme. Marliani: " Our usual life at Nohant, monotonous, peaceful and calm." Till five o'clock she taught the children. Dinner was in the open air. Some friend would come in, sometimes one and sometimes another. " In the evening, when they are gone, Chopin plays to me in the twilight. After which he falls asleep like a child, at the same time as the children."

One can still see on the wall to the left of the window in George Sand's bedroom at Nohant a date written in pencil: June 18, 1839. What does it refer to? " We may allow ourselves," writes M. W. Karenine, " for the first and only time in the course of our work, to venture into the realm of suppositions, and to imagine that on that day George Sand made a mental note of the beginning of a calm, peaceful and familiar, if not a legal intimacy, under the same roof as him whom she loved."

CHAPTER 5

For seven years, from the summer of 1839 to that of 1846, Chopin's life passed uneventfully by, in winter in Paris, in summer at Nohant — except in 1840, when neither he nor George Sand went to Nohant, so that Mme. Streicher, who had been his pupil since October 30, 1839, was able, as she tells us, to enjoy his teaching for eighteen months.

From May to October, 1839, he was at Nohant. On August 24, George Sand writes to Mme. Marliani: " Chopin is always the same, at times better, at times not so well, never exactly ill or well. I believe the poor child is fated to live permanently in a state of slight languor; fortunately his *morale* is not affected by it. As soon as he has a little strength he is gay, and when he is melancholy he turns to his piano and composes some fine page. He is giving lessons to Solange."

He himself enumerates these fine pages in a letter to Fontana. " I am composing here," he writes, " a Sonata in B flat minor, in which will be included the funeral march which you already have. There is an Allegro, then a Scherzo in E flat minor, the March and a short Finale of about three pages. After the march, the left hand discourses in unison with the right hand. I have a new Nocturne in G major. . . . You know that I have four new Mazurkas: one composed at Palma, in E minor, three here, in B major, A flat major and C sharp minor. They seem pretty to me, as their youngest children do to parents who are growing old."

While Chopin was passing the summer at Nohant, Fontana was settling his affairs in Paris. One essential piece of business was to find two apartments, one for Chopin, and another and larger one, a small house if possible, overlooking gardens, with three bedrooms, for George Sand. The novelist must have "peace and quiet, with no blacksmith in the neighbourhood. A good staircase, windows looking south, no smoke or bad smells. There are numbers of gardens in the Faubourgs St. Germain and St. Honoré. Find something splendid, quickly, and near to me." Fontana found two little houses at 16, Rue Pigalle, to be let for 2,500 francs, at the end of a garden, above the outbuildings of the main residence, which looked over the street. As for Chopin, he settled at No. 5, Rue Tronchet, in a little apartment consisting of two rooms with an entrance hall. He had asked Fontana to choose for the rooms a plain dove-grey shiny paper like the one he had had in the Chaussée d'Antin, or else dark green with two not too wide stripes. " Something different, but nice, for the hall. But if there are any prettier and more fashionable papers which are to your taste, I should like them as well, so in that case choose them. I prefer what is simple, unpretending and elegant to the garish colours of the shopkeepers." He has the grey curtains which were in his study at the Chaussée d'Antin put in the hall. The drawing-room was in red. We know that, besides the Pleyel grand on which the pupils played, there was an upright piano at which Chopin used to sit. Chopin also gave Fontana some orders for his tailor and hatter. The tailor was Dautremont. " Tell him," said Chopin, " to make me a pair of grey trousers. You can choose a dark shade of grey for winter trousers; something good, not striped, but plain and simple. You are an Englishman, so you know what I ought to have. Dautremont will be glad to know that I am coming back. I also need a black velvet waistcoat, but with very little pattern, not showy, a simple but elegant waistcoat. If he has not got any very fine velvet, let him make the waistcoat of a good silk, but not cut very low." The hatter was Duport, in the Rue de la Chaussée d'Antin. Fontana was to order him a hat. " He has my measurements and knows what I want," said Chopin. " Show him the shape hats are this year, but not too extreme."

Lastly, we know from the same source that he had a man-servant, who was paid 80 francs a month, and had to find his own food.

Having thus provided for lodgings and clothes, Chopin could return to Paris on October 11, 1839.

* * *

HE found at once that the Rue Tronchet was too far from the Rue Pigalle. He gave up his apartment to his friend Matuszyński and came to live in one of the houses rented by George Sand. Here he gave his lessons, which were over at four o'clock. This was the time at which George Sand got up. He then went up to see her. " Chopin's friends and George Sand's," writes M. Ganche, " knew and mixed with one another. " Representatives of literature, politics and finance mingled with those of music and the great world." [1]

In 1840 Chopin published the works numbered op. 35 to 41: that is to say, the Sonata in B flat minor (op. 35); the second Impromptu (op. 36); two Nocturnes (op. 37); the second Ballade (op. 38); the third Scherzo (op. 39); two Polonaises (op. 40); four Mazurkas (op. 41); the Valse in A flat major (op. 42). He also contributed to the *Méthode des Méthodes,* published by Moscheles and Fétis, three Etudes, in F minor, A flat major and D flat major.

The Sonata in B flat minor is, to use the words of Niecks, the most vigorous of Chopin's larger compositions. It is true that it is not very coherent. Schumann has pointed out the defect in its composition. " To have called this a Sonata," he says, " must be reckoned a freak, if not a piece of pride; for he has simply linked together four of his maddest children, in order to introduce them by fraud, under this name, into a place which otherwise they could perhaps never have entered." [2]

To M. Poirée, the Sonata in B flat minor, conceived during the crisis of 1838, is a poem of death, the four movements being the four cantos. " The poem — a regular epic — opens in terror. The Allegro introduces a motive with a breathless rhythm, short and abrupt — like a terrified gesture repelling us sharply — and, a calmer theme, grand and noble, rather in the style of Weber at the beginning, afterwards rising into a superb lyrical outburst."

Schumann had been struck by the moving introduction. " Only Chopin can begin like that," he says. Next comes the first motive, "stormy and passionate," as follows:

This furnishes the first four periods; then appears the second theme, M. Poirée's "idea in the style of Weber," in the relative major, D flat.

This idea is developed into a magnificent melody. It is followed by twenty breathless bars, made up of chords of the seventh, each followed by its natural resolution. Having reached this point, the whole section is repeated, with a different emotional atmosphere, but on the same plan; the first theme appears again in the left hand, while a fresh melody is sounded by the right hand; then the second theme returns, this time in B flat major, followed by this breathless development at the end, leading up "through discords, from discords to discords," to a conclusion like a hasty leave nervously taken of the listener.

"The Scherzo," says M. Poirée, "forms the second canto of the poem; again we have at the beginning a similar effect of terrifying pursuit and headlong flight. Death is prowling about a ballroom, the echoes from which reach us, sometimes quick and animated, sometimes in slackened time and with a languorous grace. And through the sweet, heart-stirring cantabile of the melody, deep voices murmur a dread psalmody on chords divided alternately between the two hands. But death has triumphed. Victorious and arrogant, he sees a whole crowd bending before him and doing him homage. . . . This triumph of death, the third section of the drama, is the wonderful funeral march, popular throughout the whole world."

The finale has been the subject of a long and violent controversy. " It is more like a piece of irony than music," writes Schumann. " And yet it must be admitted that in this unmelodic, joyless part, a certain pitiless genius breathes in our face, stuns with its heavy fist whoever tries to react against it, and compels us to listen to the end as if fascinated, and without complaint . . . but also without praise: for this is not music." The finale is characterised by a vast running passage, rather like those in one of the Etudes, but wilder. " This great movement, which sweeps the keyboard for a few minutes with its furious octaves, in unison and without appreciable form, is perhaps the boldest page which has ever been written in the whole of music. Death appears here in all the cruel realism of its brute force, which destroys and ruins all things." [3]

* * *

On April 20, 1841, Heine wrote in the *Augsburg Gazette:* " The fact that in Paris you are as it were drowned in floods of music, that there is hardly a house in which one can take refuge, as in a Noah's ark, from this deluge of sound — in fact, that the art of music has inundated our whole life: this fact is a disquieting portent to me." He attributed to this bad humour the fact that he would not write a panegyric on Liszt, who was once more back again in Paris, and whom the great world, " especially the hysterical great world of the ladies," surrounded with enthusiastic admiration and frenzied applause. Heine added: " All other pianists are eclipsed beside him, with a single exception: Chopin, the Raphael of the pianoforte." [4] Chopin had given no concerts in Paris since 1832.[5] He liked playing before a few friends only. " A small circle of chosen listeners, who, he believed, had a real desire to hear him, was the only thing which would persuade him to approach the piano. But then, what emotions he was able to arouse! In what ardent and melancholy reveries he loved to pour forth his soul! It was about midnight, as a rule, that he would abandon himself most completely. Then, in obedience to the mute prayer of some fine, speaking eyes, he became a poet. . . ." Thus speaks Berlioz.

In 1841, however, Chopin resolved to give a concert, which took place on April 26 at the Salle Pleyel. Liszt gave an enthusiastic account of it in the *Gazette musicale* of May 2: " Last Monday, at eight in the evening, M. Pleyel's Rooms were splendidly lit up; an unending series of equipages kept bearing to the foot of a staircase, covered with a carpet and perfumed with flowers, the most elegant women, the most fashionable young men, the most famous artists, the richest financiers, the most illustrious noblemen, the whole *élite* of society, a whole aristocracy of birth, fortune, talent and beauty.

" A grand piano stood open on a platform; everybody was crowding round it, vying with one another for the nearest seats; even before he began, everybody was listening with concentrated attention, saying to one another that they must not lose a single chord, intention or idea of him who was to come and take his seat there."

Chopin's success was complete, and henceforward his

fame was undisputed. "His exquisite repute," says Liszt, "has remained untouched by any attack. Criticism has remained absolutely silent before it, as if posterity were already present; and in the whole of the brilliant audience which rallied to the poet, who had remained too long silent, there was not a single reserve or restriction; all mouths were full of the same praise."

In June Chopin and George Sand went to Nohant. Life flowed peacefully on. There were a few pleasant guests at Nohant, among them Mme. Pauline Viardot. "I feel as calm and serene as a swaddled baby," writes Chopin. We know from his correspondence with Fontana that he had just composed for Schlesinger, the publisher, a twenty-fifth Prelude in C sharp minor, which alone constitutes op. 45. He reckoned upon giving it to Macchetti to bring out in Vienna, for the price of 300 francs.

It is hard not to be struck with the difference between the prelude of op. 45 and those of op. 28, which had preceded it by two years. The former has something agonised, choking and breathless about it. It begins with an introduction in chords of the sixth.

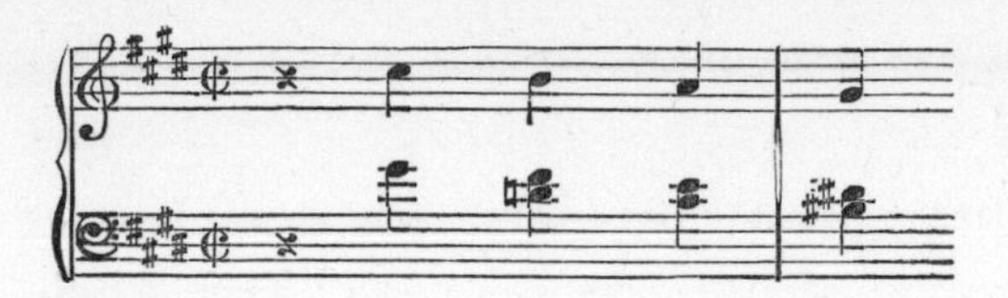

ending with a very expressive appoggiatura on the tonic.

Immediately afterwards we hear the call of the dominant G sharp. It is the opening note of a period, which begins as follows:

Next comes a period of five bars, like the introduction — inspired by it, indeed — but still with this character of breathlessness and appeal; next an imitation of the first period. A new melody then strikes in, akin indeed to that of the first period and the introduction, but less breathless, firmer and fuller. It forms a period of seven bars. Next the insistent cry of the first theme returns once again. This motive, or cry, is repeated eight times, passing from one key to another, and leads up to a repetition of the second theme, first in A major, then in F. This alternation of arresting figures with melodies is most characteristic of Chopin. Then a sort of silence falls. The left hand, which is still in F, sketches the chord listlessly. It is as though the composer were only disengaging himself slowly from his dream. He requires a bridge of another four bars to rise chromatically from F to G.[6] At last he returns to the key of C sharp minor. He repeats the first period. He touches, as it were, softly the key of G sharp minor, for which he has a great affection, and returns to C sharp minor by a cadence which is no more than a long and subtle modulation. Twice is heard the call of the principal motive. But in the midst of this plaint, we feel as if his personality were reduplicated. Side by side with the suffering spirit there is in him a spirit which consoles, and its eternal unrest is lulled throughout the rest of the piece in the yielding embrace of an accompaniment of arpeggi.

Schlesinger and Macchetti both bought this prelude. They published it in November, together with the Polonaise (op. 44) in F sharp minor.

But there is one rather moving fact: there is an evident kinship between the Prelude and the Polonaise. In both there are the same agony, the same cries of appeal. Did some drama take place during this winter of 1840–1841 of which we are unaware, and of which these two pieces are the mysterious witnesses which alone reveal it to us?

Liszt has described this Polonaise in his usual spirited vein, interpreting it rather in terms of the outer world, as he always does. He is a man who would take heart-beats for cannon-fire. "It is," he says, "as it were a dream told at the end of a sleepless night by the earliest rays of a grey and dreary winter dawn. . . . The principal motive is vehement, with a sinister feeling like the period preceding a hurricane; the ear imagines that it can catch exasperated cries, like a challenge thrown down to all the elements. Immediately after this we hear the note of the tonic recurring incessantly at the beginning of every bar, like repeated cannon-fire, or like a hotly contested battle in the distance. This note is followed, bar after bar, by a sequence of strange chords. We know of nothing in the works of the greatest composers like the striking effect produced by this passage, suddenly interrupted by a pastoral scene, by a mazurka in idyllic style which almost seems to diffuse a fragrance of mint and marjoram! But far from effacing the remembrance of the deep feeling of misery which took possession of us at the beginning, on the contrary, by a bitter and ironical contrast, it increases the painful emotions of the hearer to such a pitch that he is almost relieved when the first phrase returns. . . . Like a dream, this improvisation comes to an end with no conclusion save a dreary, shuddering passage, which leaves the soul subdued by its impression of poignant misery."

The following are the passages referred to by Liszt:

The Polonaise, which is in F sharp minor, starts with a period of eight bars, serving as an introduction. A second period contains that hectic motive which Liszt calls the principal theme, and which we will call motive A. It runs as follows:

A third period, this time of ten bars, gives out the motive for the second time in the bass, with a countermelody in the right hand. A fourth period gives out a fresh theme, which we may call motive B, this time in B flat minor.

This exposition of a series of themes in a corresponding number of periods following one after another is an artless device habitual with Chopin, whose powers of melodic invention are inexhaustible, but who has little taste for academic development. He confines himself to repeating A with certain pianistic variants, returning to the motive B in B flat minor. A third repetition of A leads us into A major. Then begins a fresh subject — the one which impressed Liszt by its repetition of the tonic, followed by strange chords. This motive, which we shall call C, has indeed something of a martial effect:

It is repeated for twenty bars with fierce insistence; then interrupted by a repetition of motive B in C sharp minor, when it starts off again for thirteen bars; then, dying away in a pianissimo in A minor, it suddenly gives way to that graceful mazurka rhythm (theme D) in which Liszt found a fragrance of mint and marjoram; and in truth the whole piece has the dramatic incoherence of a dream.

These two pieces were finished when Chopin arrived at Nohant in June, 1841. We see that he finished here the Tarantella in A flat major (op. 43). Fontana copied it out, after making sure, by reference to Rossini's Tarantella in F, that it ought really to be written in 6/8 and not in 12/8 time, nor in four time with triplets. A little later, Chopin likewise sent Fontana the Allegro de concert (op. 46), some Nocturnes (op. 48), the third Ballade (op. 47) and the Fantaisie (op. 49). It was Fontana who negotiated with the publishers, against whom Chopin protected himself energetically. All these works, from op. 43 to 49, appeared during this year. Three Mazurkas (op. 50) also appeared in November, 1841.

* * *

On February 21, 1842, Chopin gave another concert at the Salle Pleyel. "At M. Pleyel's Rooms," wrote *La France musicale,* "Chopin gave a delightful evening concert, a festive occasion graced by sweet smiles, soft rosy faces, little white, shapely hands; a magnificent festivity, in which simplicity was wedded to grace and elegance, and good taste served as a pedestal to wealth. Gold ribbons, pale blue gauze, strings of quivering pearls, the freshest roses and pinks, a thousand varied hues, as pretty and gay as could be, were grouped and mingled in every way on the perfumed tresses and silvery shoulders of the loveliest women, whom princely houses vie with each other to entertain." George Sand was there with her daughter, and no doubt with her young cousin Augustine Brault. Every eye was turned towards her. She bent her head and smiled.

Chopin played his latest works: the third Ballade, the three Mazurkas in A flat, B major and A minor, the three Etudes in A flat, F minor and C minor, the Prelude in D flat, the Impromptu in G, and four Nocturnes. Mme. Viardot sang, and Franchomme played the violoncello.

The summer of 1842 was spent as usual at Nohant. Delacroix, who was a guest there that year, wrote on June 22: " I have endless tête-à-tête conversations with Chopin. I am very fond of him and he is a man of rare distinction." And again: " From time to time there are wafted to you through the window opening on the garden bursts of Chopin's music as he works there; all this is mingled with the song of nightingales and the perfume of roses." [7]

In the autumn, when they returned to Paris, Chopin and George Sand left the Rue Pigalle, and went to live in two adjacent apartments, Nos. 5 and 9 in the Square d'Orléans. Mme. Marliani was already living at No. 7. " She lived in a fine apartment," writes George Sand, " between our two. We had only to cross a large sanded court with plants in it, which was always well kept, in order to meet, sometimes in her apartment, sometimes in mine, sometimes in Chopin's, when he was in the mood to make music. We all dined together with her, sharing the expense. It was a very good combination. . . . Chopin was glad, too, to have a fine separate sitting-room to which he could retire to compose or dream. But he was fond of society, and hardly availed himself of his sanctum except for giving lessons. It was only at Nohant that he created and wrote."[8]

There is nothing to mention during the year 1843. We only know that in September they made an excursion to the banks of the Creuse. "I am just back from a little expedition to the banks of the Creuse," writes George Sand, "across very low mountains, which are, however, very picturesque and much more inaccessible than the Alps, for there are neither roads nor inns. Chopin climbed everywhere on his donkey; he slept on straw, and was never better than during these risks and fatigues."[9]

On April 20, 1842, Chopin had lost his friend Matuszyński, who died of consumption;[10] on May 3, 1844, he lost his father, Nicholas Chopin, who was seventy-five years of age. "The death of his friend and of his father," says George Sand, "were two terrible blows to him. He was visibly wasting away, and I did not know what medicines to use in order to combat his increasing nervous irritation." Chopin's eldest sister, Louise Jendrzejewicz, had come to France with her husband, and George Sand invited them to Nohant. "You will find my dear child very sickly and changed since the time you last saw him, but do not be too much alarmed for his health. It has been the same, with no general alteration, for the last six years, during which I have seen him every day. A rather severe fit of coughing every morning, two or three more serious attacks every winter, lasting no more than two or three days each, a little suffering from neuralgia from time to time, that is his usual condition. For the rest, his chest is healthy and there is no definite lesion in his delicate organisation. I still hope that he will grow stronger in time, but I am sure, at least, that he will last as long as anyone else, with a regular life and care. But the joy of seeing you, though mingled with deep and sorrowful emotions, which will perhaps upset him a little the first day, will do him a great deal of good, and I am so glad for his sake that I bless the decision you have made."

The Jendrzejewicz family passed the month of August at Nohant, and in September Chopin took his sister back to Paris. On the 18th George Sand wrote to

Mme. Jendrzejewicz: "We live on you alone since your departure. Frederick has suffered from the separation, as you may well believe, but his health has borne the strain fairly well. In fact, your kind and pious resolution to come has borne good fruit. It has freed his soul from all bitterness and made him strong and courageous. One cannot enjoy such happiness for a month without some trace of it remaining. . . . I assure you that you are the best doctor he has ever had, for it suffices for me to speak to him about you to bring back his love of living." It would seem that Mme. Jendrzejewicz had exercised a soothing influence on the relations between George Sand and Chopin. Chopin had had scruples on the score of his liaison, and many of the ideas of his anticlerical and democratic mistress must have exasperated him. Now George Sand wrote to Mme. Marliani after Louise had left them: "Thanks to his sister, who is much more advanced than he is, Chopin has now recovered from all his prejudices. It is a remarkable conversion, which he has not noticed himself."

In the *Augsburg Gazette* of March 28, 1843, Heine drew an amusing picture of the pianists of Paris. Alexandre Dreyschok, the Bohemian pianist, had won a triumph by banging like a deaf man. "Hang yourself,

CHOPIN'S SISTERS

LOUISE JENDRZEJEWICZ
From an oil painting by Ziemiecki

ISABELLA BARCINSKA
From an oil painting by Miroszewski

Franz Liszt," writes Heine, " you are nothing but a second-rate blower compared to this Aeolus, who binds hurricanes together like birch-twigs and thrashes the sea's back with them." Heine adds that the older pianists are gradually falling into oblivion and expiating the exaggerated successes of their youth. " Kalkbrenner alone to some extent maintains his standing. He appeared in public again this winter, at the concert of one of his lady pupils; an embalmed smile still plays round his lips, like that which we noticed the other day on an Egyptian Pharaoh whose mummy was being unwrapped in a room at the Paris Museum." Then follow the most malicious anecdotes, ending with a dig at Kalkbrenner's conventional costume, " his elegant dress, all spick and span, his refined and distinguished manners. I say distinguished, though they are only affected, and a careful observer can frequently distinguish, mingled with his conversation, Berlin vernacular of the most vulgar kind, pointing to the very lowest extraction." [11]

Next comes a paragraph about Pixis, a contemporary of Kalkbrenner, as to whom " nobody knew whether he was still alive, or indeed, had ever lived." [12] Edward Wolff was prolific and full of life. Stephen Heller was more of a composer than a virtuoso, a true artist without affectation or exaggeration, a romantic soul in a classical form. Thalberg had been in Paris for two months, and was not to give a concert, but would play that week at the concert of one of his friends. His execution was perfectly " gentleman-like, perfectly easy and correct." " There is only one pianist whom I prefer to him: Chopin, though it is true that he is rather a composer than a virtuoso. When I am near Chopin, I quite forget his mastery of piano technique, and plunge into the soft abysses of his music, into the mingled pain and delight of his creations, which are as tender as they are profound. Chopin is the great tone-poet of genius, the artist who should only be named in company with Mozart, Beethoven, Rossini or Berlioz." [13]

A year later, on April 25, 1844, Heine writes: " I am forced to keep repeating that there are only three pianists worthy of serious notice; these are, in the first place Chopin, the enchanting poet-musician, who has unfortunately been very ill this winter, and is seldom visible to the public." [14] The two others were Thalberg and " our very good friend Liszt, who is at present once more causing a stir in the great world of Paris." The winter of 1844–1845 was an extremely hard one, and no doubt aggravated Chopin's malady. In June,

1845, he returned to Nohant. In a letter to his family of October 1st, 1845, it suddenly becomes clear that he realised the menace hanging over him. "They write to me from Paris that Artot the violinist is dead. That great strong fellow, with his broad shoulders and big bones, died of consumption at Ville d'Avray a few weeks ago. . . . Nobody would have guessed who saw us both together that he would die first, and of consumption too." This sentiment, which is so frequent in those condemned to death, this unconscious habit of drawing confidence from the deaths of others, appears repeatedly. On December 24, 1845, after his return to Paris, he writes: "I have already outlived so many who were younger and stronger than I, that I feel as if I were immortal." He had but four years more to live.

* * *

What works were published by Chopin in the years between 1842 and 1845? We left him at the end of 1841 at op. 50. In order to understand the arrangement of his publications, we must remember that he only composed during the summer. The normal thing was for the works composed during one summer to appear in the course of the following winter. We see this in the case of op. 51, which is the third Impromptu, and the fourth Ballade (op. 52). They appeared in February, 1843, and no doubt represent the work which he did during the summer of 1842. In like manner the works composed during the summer of 1843 appeared in December of that year; these were the eighth Polonaise (op. 53) and the fourth Scherzo (op. 54).

In 1844 everything was changed. Chopin was to publish his works in the height of the summer. Are we to see in this a result of Franchomme's intervention? For from this year onwards he took Fontana's place in the negotiations with publishers.[15] The two Nocturnes constituting op. 55, the three Mazurkas constituting op. 56, came out in Germany in August. But in the autumn of 1844, after his sister's departure, he had finished a more considerable work, the Sonata in B minor. This time he published it at the height of the Parisian season, just before his departure for Nohant in June, 1845, at the same time as the Berceuse. These two works form his ops. 57 (Berceuse) and 58 (Sonata). We must pause for an instant to consider them.

The sonata in B minor forms the subject of a study by M. Vincent d'Indy,[16] and it will suffice to condense his analysis of it here. " It is unfortunately quite lacking in constructive power and coördination of ideas," writes the composer of *Fervaal,* " but most of the actual ideas are truly brilliant in wealth of melodic invention."

The sonata is in four movements. The first is an Allegro maestoso in B minor. The first theme, says M. d'Indy, has a stamp of true nobility, with symphonic qualities which a Beethoven would certainly have turned to great advantage.

" But," continues M. d'Indy, " the composer is unfortunately unable to pursue the exposition of his idea with equal success; he has recourse to useless repetitions, to mere arbitrary juxtapositions of four bars here and four bars there, without cohesion either of melody or of tonality." We have frequently indicated these juxtapositions of four-bar phrases in Chopin's longer works. After a " fairly well-handled bridge-passage," corresponding with what we have called the " transition group," we arrive at the second subject, M. d'Indy's theme B, in D major.

This theme B is itself subdivided into three phrases, says M. d'Indy. By phrase the celebrated author of the

Traité de composition musicale here understands a series of periods based upon different ideas. Here is the first period of phrase b′:

This period is followed by another one, loaded with Italianisms and ornaments, about which M. d'Indy is very severe.[17] He is even more so about the development section, " a regular student's exercise by a student who has decided to introduce a development here, because it is the custom to do so; but all logic is jealously banished from it." Lastly, the final recapitulation is practically non-existent, for the fine motive of the theme group [theme A] is not repeated, and only the second subject is repeated in its entirety in the key of B major.

" A childish sketch," concludes M. d'Indy. On the other hand, the Scherzo is altogether charming. The third movement, a Largo in B major, is a lied in the usual form, in which the opening theme has again an Italian character, but in which " the central section has all the caressing grace of the author's best works."

Finally, in the finale, which is in rondo form with a thrice-repeated refrain, " the nervous and attractive invalid with whom we are acquainted gives way to a vigorous and powerful creature. It is as though the materials for this fine piece had been hewn with an axe by some carpenter who had only roughed out the joints; but these awkwardnesses of construction, though they do no serious harm to the finale, give it, on the other hand, a somewhat rough appearance."

The productions of 1845 are limited to three Mazurkas, which he announces in a letter to his family of July 20.[18] They appeared before December 12, for he writes on that day: " My new mazurkas have come out in Berlin, at Stern's." He adds in the same letter that he would like to finish a Sonata for piano and violoncello, a Barcarolle " and another piece besides, for which I cannot think of a name; I doubt whether I shall have time, for the rush is already beginning." However, he seems actually to have finished the Sonata for piano and violoncello, for he adds on the 24th: " I have been trying over a little with Franchomme a sonata for 'cello, and it is going well. I do not know whether I shall have time to get it printed this year." Whether he finished them or not, these works did not in fact appear that winter. The summer of 1846 had also to pass by, and it was not till September, 1846, that the Barcarolle (op. 60) was published, together with that work without a title which became the Polonaise fantaisie (op. 61). As to the Sonata for piano and 'cello, dedicated to Franchomme, it did not appear till October, 1847, as op. 65.

CHAPTER 6

LET us pause a moment at the end of 1845, which we have now reached. The twilight is beginning for the poor artist. Let us seize this moment to try and define the genius of this enchanter, the Ariel among pianists, as he was called.

After the concert of February 21, 1842, the *Gazette musicale* alluded to this personality, of which nobody else possessed the secret, and which inspired Chopin's playing. "... The keyboard becomes as it were transformed, turning almost into a new instrument, as it obeys the fevered impulse of a tender and passionate genius. Liszt and Thalberg, as we know, call forth transports of passion: Chopin arouses them too, but of a less vehement and clamorous nature, for the very reason that it is a more intimate fibre, a gentler emotion which he stirs in the heart." [1]

Let us first look for the secret of his technique in his teaching. The traditions collected by Kleczyński are as follows:

For Chopin, delicacy of touch was the basis of instruction. The first condition for a good touch was a good position of the hand, and he was very exacting on this point. " He trained the hand with infinite care before entrusting the reproduction of musical ideas to it. In order to give the hand a position at once graceful and convenient (two qualities which, in his opinion, always went together) he would make his pupil drop it lightly on the keyboard, in such a way that the five fingers rested upon the notes E, F sharp, G sharp, A sharp, B. This was for him the normal position." [2]

In this position he would make them play five-finger exercises, to ensure the evenness and independence of the fingers, first with a light staccato touch, next with a heavier one, then legato but accentuated, lastly with a complete legato. The following is the scheme of the exercises:

He made them do corresponding exercises in the left hand, placing it in the position F, G flat, A flat, B flat and C.

They next worked at scales, bearing in mind that the hand must be maintained in its normal position. He began with scales in which this normal position naturally occurs, B major for the right hand, D flat major for the left hand. He attached far more importance to the maintenance of this position than to passing the thumb. It sometimes occurred that he passed it under the fourth finger, or even the fifth. The following, for instance, is a fingering taken from the B minor Scherzo.

And here is another, taken from the Etude in A minor:

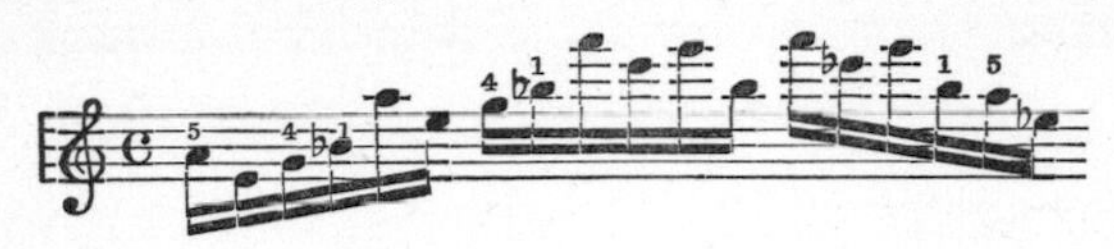

These fingerings, which scandalised pianists of the old school, left the hand in position. The same is true of certain instances of passing the third or fourth finger over the fifth. Here is an example from the Nocturne in B flat minor.

The study of the scales and arpeggios was first carried out staccato, and, as we have said, in the scales of B natural and D flat. " Then, by the various gradations of mezzo staccato, of accentuated staccato, etc. . . . lifting the fingers high, and by the mere play of the muscles, they arrived at passing the thumb without allowing the hand to lose its horizontal position; next the hand was allowed to proceed to more difficult scales, to arpeggio passages, in which even very wide intervals are stretched as they occur, without effort, and even without lifting the fingers very high. I know by experience that by this means one arrives at an even and sure touch." [3]

Chopin made all his pupils work at the second volume of Clementi's *Preludes and Exercises*, especially the first exercise in A flat. "Every toneless or hard note had to be repeated, and was pointed out severely. To complete his distress, at the very outset the pupil met with an arpeggio which has caused many tears.[4] It had to be played crescendo, rapidly, but not abruptly. It was this arpeggio which brought down upon a pupil a somewhat too hasty exclamation from the master, who bounded in his chair, crying, 'What is that? Was it a dog that barked just now?' This luckless study had to be worked at in every manner: it was played fast, slow, loud, soft, staccato and legato, until the touch became even, delicate and light without being weak." [5] Next he made them work at Clementi's *Gradus ad Parnassum*, and lastly at J. S. Bach's *Wohltemperirte Klavier*.

It is a controversial point whether Chopin held his hand flat or not. The cast of his hand, showing the first joint of the thumb definitely bent and the other fingers curved, and about to touch the keys with the cushion at the tip of the finger, seems to point to the contrary.
The question of touch is closely akin to that of legato, which seems to have been the very soul of Chopin's playing. His pupil Mme. Streicher writes: " He took infinite pains to teach his pupils to play legato and how to play cantabile. His most severe criticism was ' He (or she) cannot play two notes legato.' "
There is a very delicate question concerned with the free rhythm known as *tempo rubato*. This latitude in time had already been employed by Beethoven in his later works. He indicates *rubato* in the Trio op. 97 and the Sonata op. 106. Mendelssohn relates that Mme. Ertmann, to whom the Sonata op. 101 was dedicated, used to play it in this spirit. Liszt has left a charming description of Chopin's rubato:
" In his playing," he says, " the great artist rendered enchantingly that sort of emotional trepidation, timid or breathless, which seizes the heart when one believes oneself to be in the neighbourhood of supernatural beings . . . He always made the melody undulate like a light boat borne on the bosom of a mighty billow; or

else he would give it a wavering motion, like an aerial apparition suddenly arising in this tangible and palpable world. In his writings he indicates this manner, which gave such a peculiar stamp to his virtuosity in the first place, by the words *tempo rubato:* stolen, broken time, at once supple, abrupt and languishing, quivering like a flame beneath the breath which stirs it, like a cornfield rippling under the soft pressure of a warm breeze, like treetops bent hither and thither at the whim of a capricious gust.

" But this expression, which explained nothing to those who knew, meant nothing to those who did not. . . . Later on, Chopin gave up adding this indication to his music, being convinced that for those who understood it, it was impossible not to divine this rule of irregularity. So all his compositions ought to be played with this kind of accentual and prosodic lilt, this *morbidezza,* the secret of which it was hard to grasp when one had not heard him in person. He seemed anxious to teach this style to his many pupils, especially to his fellow-countrymen, to whom above all others he desired to impart the spirit of his inspiration. They, or rather his countrywomen, grasped it with that aptitude which they have for all that concerns sentiment and poetry." [6]

Tempo rubato, then, is a free prosody, flexible as the rhythms of life and of thought, and not at all a suppression of the beat. It would also be an error to make it insipid, instead of giving it its living character. Chopin insisted upon strict rhythm, writes Mme. Streicher, hated languor, dragging the time and misplaced rubato as much as he did an exaggerated ritardando. "Pray be seated," he said one day with gentle mockery to one of these languishing pianists. Georges Mathias is even more explicit: "Chopin often insisted," he writes, "upon the observance of strict time in that part of the music which formed the accompaniment, simultaneously with a freedom of expression in the melodic part, which should admit of a modification of the time." [7] Such was Chopin as a pianist.[8] But as a virtuoso he was no different from what he was as a composer, and this may begin to help us to understand him. The secrets of his piano playing can be recognised in his music. His *legato* finds its counterpart in the smooth transitions found in his works. He constantly makes use of delayed effects and appoggiaturas, which cause one chord to melt into the next. Comparing him with his contemporaries, one is struck by his highly-developed use of harmonic sequences which are merely fused and, as it were, imperceptible progressions, a sort of *legato* in the handling of transitions. In his melody we find that throb of life which is reflected in his *tempo rubato*. There is a kind of music which appears to be hewn in stone; but his quivers like willow-leaves in the sun. That independence of the parts which was apparent in his playing, leaving the melody free within the bounds of a strict rhythm, is equally recognisable in his music. When we analyse it, we are astonished at the strict form of the periods. There is no music more square than Chopin's, but there is likewise none which is more fluid and aerial.

Everywhere in his works we may find this co-existence of two systems, amounting, we may say, to a sort of contradiction, which Liszt would no doubt have attributed to the Slav character. Chopin is never in harmony with himself. He is both sad and gay at the same moment. His melancholy suddenly gives way to an outburst of passion. In the midst of a cantilena passage he is seized with a rush of frenzy. He is unstable, wavering, transparent and variable.

Liszt divided Chopin's works into three periods: the first, to which belong the Etudes, is characterised by an exuberant youthful ardour; next come his more elaborate, finished and self-conscious works; and finally a last period, strange and tormented, in which

George Sand
From a drawing by Alfred de Musset

Chopin
From a drawing by George Sand

his melancholy becomes a morbid irascibility, a hectic trembling. "Almost stifled by the oppression of his controlled violence, he now only used his art to reflect to himself his own tragedy; having begun by making melody of his emotions, he now set to work to dissect them. . . . Chopin's melody now became tortuous; his restless nervous impressionability led him to remodel his motives with implacable persistence, as painful to witness as the tortures arising from those maladies of soul or body which can only be healed by death." [9] Without pushing this classification too far, we may indeed recognise in the youthful works a more exclusively brilliant style; next comes a phase in which art and poetry have arrived at a happy pitch of perfection; and lastly the poignant works of his latter days. George Sand has left a speaking portrait of the composer. "His creative power was spontaneous, miraculous," she says. "It came to him without effort or warning. It would come to him at the piano, sudden, complete and sublime, or else it would sing in his head while he was walking, and he would hasten to make it audible to himself by throwing it on to the instrument. But then began the most heart-rending labour which I have ever witnessed. It was a series of efforts, of fits of irresolution and impatience to recover certain details of the theme which he had tried over; he conceived a melody as a whole, but when he tried to write it down he analysed it too much, and his regret at not recovering it in a clear-cut form plunged him, by his own account, into a sort of despair. He would shut himself up in his room for whole days, weeping, pacing up and down, breaking his pens, repeating and modifying one bar a hundred times, writing it down and blotting it out equally often, and starting again the next day with a minute and despairing perseverance. He would spend six weeks over a page, only to end by writing it out in the end just as he had sketched it in the original draft." [10]

NOTES TO PART THREE

[1] "Mme. Sand at this time often heard this most exceptional artist talked about by a friend of Chopin's, a musician, one of those who had hailed his arrival in Paris with the greatest joy." F. Liszt, *op. cit.*, p. 251.

[2] *Op. cit.*, pp. 146 sq.

[3] This refers to Mallefille, who was George Sand's lover.

[4] Gutmann was born at Heidelberg and was just nineteen.

[1] W. Karenine, *George Sand, sa vie et ses oeuvres*, t. III, (1912), p. 32.

[2] This letter was published by W. Karenine, *op. cit.*, p. 42.

[3] *Op. cit.*, III, pp. 44–53.

[4] This interruption seems significant. Chopin had, however, some works in his portfolios. They were the ones that he played to Schumann in September, 1836, at Leipzig, and that the latter enumerated in his letter to Dorn: the second Ballade (in its first state), some nocturnes, études and mazurkas, almost everything that he published at the end of 1837.

[5] *Op. cit.*, III, pp. 257–258.

[1] The earliest alarms about Chopin's health seem to date from 1836. We have seen the anxious advice given him by the Wodzińskis. During the winter of 1836–1837, he had influenza again. This is what he says himself in a letter to Anthony Wodziński, published by Szulc. During the summer of 1837 they wanted to send him to Ems, but he was too ill to move.

[2] On January 15, George Sand writes: "Chopin is playing on a bad Majorcan piano, which reminds me of Bouffé's in *Pauvre Jacques*." On the 22nd: "The only event worthy of note since my last letter is the arrival of the expected piano. At last it has been landed safely, and the vaulted cells of the Charterhouse are enlivened by it." They had had to wrangle with the Customs House officials for three weeks, and pay a duty of 300 francs.

[3] F. Liszt, *op. cit.*, p. 273. Shortly before this (p. 239) Liszt quotes some fine verses by Count Zaluski on this same prelude. But Zaluski sees in this prelude, with its animation and passion, succeeded by a melancholy calm, a picture of the sea, the forest and the storms of the heart, and not a reminiscence of the storm in the Balearic Islands at all. He would find this reminiscence in No. 19, in E flat minor, with raindrops falling through rays of sunshine. The sky darkens, the storm breaks, then the sun shines out again, once more darkened by the rain.

[4] Chopin requested Fontana to pay back the 1,000 francs lent him by Leo the banker at the moment of his departure, and speaks of him in no measured terms.

[5] Strictly speaking, the second period apparently consists of thirteen bars, but one of them, the third from the end, is merely a melancholy suspension of the thought at the moment of conclusion.

[6] Probst had retired from publishing since 1834; all Chopin's works after op. 15 had been published by Breitkopf, except the Bolero (op. 19) published by Peters. It is not known why he wanted to leave Breitkopf and go back to Probst.

[7] This quotation is from *L'histoire de ma vie*, IV, p. 443 and was consequently written a long time afterwards. We must not forget that George Sand always represented that in Majorca Chopin was ill in consequence of his own nerves rather than of the climate and discomfort. For her part, she would gladly have spent two or three years there alone with her children. This optimism exonerates her from blame for having dragged Chopin into this fatal journey.

[1] This passage was published for the first time by M. W. Karenine, *op. cit.*, III, p. 98.

[1] E. Ganche, *op. cit.*, 5th ed. (1921), p. 251.

[2] *Op. cit.*, III, p. 51.

[3] E. Poirée, *op. cit.*, p. 118.

[4] H. Heine, *Lutezia*, pp. 186–187.

[5] On October 29, 1839, he had been invited to Saint-Cloud with Moscheles. "Chopin, who was applauded and admired as a favourite, played some Nocturnes and Etudes," reported Moscheles the day after. He then improvised on Grisar's *La Folle.*

[6] Passing through the keys of F major, B major, G sharp minor, C sharp minor.

[7] Chopin for his part wrote to Franchomme on August 30, 1845: "Delacroix is the most admirable artist whom one could meet; I have spent delightful hours with him. He adores Mozart and knows all his operas by heart."

[8] This fact is confirmed by Chopin himself, who writes to his people from Nohant on October 1, 1845: "I must, however, finish a few manuscripts before leaving this place, for it is impossible for me to compose in the winter."

[9] Letter to Mme. Marliani, October 2, 1843.

[10] The date of Matuszynski's death was established by F. Hoesick, *Chopin*, II, p. 444.

[11] H. Heine, *Lutezia*, pp. 313–314.

[12] Pixis was born at Mannheim in 1788, and settled in Paris in 1825. Chopin had met him at Stuttgart. He gives a funny account in a letter of December 25, 1831, of the fit of jealousy which Pixis had when Chopin met on the stairs a pretty girl of sixteen who was living with Pixis in Paris. Chopin imitated him so cleverly that one day, when Nowadowski was in a box near the real Pixis, he thought it was Chopin, and asked him to stop his mimicry.

[13] Heine, *Lutezia*, pp. 316–317.

[14] *Ibid.*, p. 392.

[15] Fontana had sailed for Havana, where he married. He did not return to France till after Chopin's death, about 1852.

[16] Vincent d'Indy, *Cours de composition musicale*, II, p. 407 sq.

[17] "This defect is very frequent in Chopin, when he attempts forms demanding a certain grandeur of conception. He then has recourse to an Italian turn of phrase, borrowed from those

fashionable in the theatres and drawing-rooms of his day." Schumann, in analysing the Sonata in B flat minor (op. 35) had already recalled Chopin's liking for Bellini, and pointed out "a slight incursion into the south." For Chopin's Italianisms, see J. Chantavoine, *Musiciens et poètes*, Paris, 1912.

[18] "I have written three new mazurkas; they will probably be published in Berlin, for a nice fellow of my acquaintance, Stern, a professional musician, begged them of me for his father, who is opening a music-shop."

[1] *Gazette musicale*, February 27, 1842.

[2] J. Kleczynski, *op. cit.*, pp. 38–39.

[3] J. Kleczynski, *op. cit.*, pp. 41–42.

[4] 

[5] *Ibid.*, pp. 46–47.

[6] F. Liszt, *op. cit.*, pp. 115–116. Cf. F. Hoesick, *op. cit.*, III, p. 311 sq.

[7] This is what Chopin meant when he said: "Let your left hand act as conductor and always keep time." Such liberty, even with this restriction, none the less scandalised Berlioz. "Chopin bore with impatience the curb of strict time," he says; "in my opinion he carried rhythmical independence much too far."

[8] The Conservatoire library possesses a copy of Chopin's works which belonged to Mlle. O'Meara, with pencil notes in the master's hand. They are cited by M. Ed. Ganche, *op. cit.*, p. 202–210. In it will be found, for instance, successive notes struck with the same finger (the three first notes of the Nocturne in C minor are struck with the third finger). On the other hand, we must

remember that our instruments sustain the sound better, which is bound to modify the hints on pedalling, as Kleczynski points out, and the tempi, as Kullak considers.

[9] F. Liszt, *op. cit.*, pp. 25–26.

[10] George Sand, *Histoire de ma vie*, IV, pp. 470–471. This is a partial testimony. George Sand, who wrote as an ox ploughs, was ill able to understand these agonies, and exasperated Chopin by attempting to tear him from them. But Liszt also speaks of "his studious patience in elaborating and perfecting his works." F. Liszt, *op. cit.*, p. 198.

PART FOUR

THE DEATH AGONY

1846–1849

CHAPTER 1

IN 1846 a breach between Chopin and George Sand was already impending.

That year, like the previous ones, had been spent by Chopin at Nohant. But on June 25 the *Courrier français* began publishing *Lucrezia Floriani.* George Sand had drawn herself in the person of Lucrezia, an actress tired of life and disillusioned in love. She had represented Chopin in the person of Prince Karol.

Prince Karol, delicate both in body and mind, with a charming, sexless beauty, was " something like those ideal creatures with which the poetry of the Middle Ages used to adorn Christian churches; an angel, fair of face as a tall, sad woman, pure and slender in form as a young god of Olympus, and, to crown this union of qualities, an expression at once tender and severe, at once chaste and passionate. Nothing could be at once purer and more elevated than his thoughts, nothing could exceed the tenacity and exclusiveness of his affections or his devotion even in the smallest trifles." [1]

When Lucrezia meets Karol, she is wearied by fifteen

years of passion, and believes that she has renounced love. She nevertheless yields to him, but her sentiment is almost a maternal one. " I will love him," she said, covering the young prince's pale brow with a long, firm kiss, " but it will be as his mother loved him." George Sand adds that it was Providence who had sent Karol the person most capable of helping and saving him. It was Lucrezia again, " who had protected and rehabilitated, saved or attempted to save the men whom she had dearly loved. Tenderly chiding their vices, devotedly atoning for their faults, she had almost made gods of these mere mortals. But she had sacrificed herself too completely to succeed."

Karol simply could not understand such a nature. He hated in Lucrezia " what in his own mind he called a background of bohemian free-and-easiness, a certain hardness and commonness of nature. So far was he from taking alarm at the pain he gave her, that he assured himself of her insensibility, saying to himself that she had moments of solicitude due to her kindness, but that, as a rule, nothing could affect a nature so strong and full of resisting power, so easy to distract or to console. At these times one might almost have thought that he was jealous of his mistress's very health, which appeared to be so strong, and blamed

God for the calm with which he had endowed her." The worst of it was that this ferocious egoist was superlatively polite and reserved, so that " one could never so much as suspect what was going on within him. The more exasperated he was, the colder he appeared. At these times he was truly unbearable. They prompted him to indulge his wit, a spurious, brilliant wit with which he would torture those whom he loved. He was mocking, stiff, affected, and bored with everything. It was as if he took pleasure in biting gently, though the wound which he made reached the very vitals. Or if he had not the heart to contradict and scoff, he would retire into a disdainful silence, or heartrending sulks." It was only when Lucrezia was so overcome as to admit how she was suffering that he would become charming once more. " Karol's tender affection was at once revived, he forgot his bad temper and became excessively alarmed. He would wait on her on bended knee, and at such times he adored her even more than he had done during their honeymoon." Lucrezia ends by dying of Karol's treatment of her.

George Sand assures us not only that she had not intended to represent Chopin, but that he did not even recognise himself in Karol. It was not till after the rupture that " enemies persuaded him that this novel was a revelation of his character." But even admitting that the novel was not a cause of the rupture, it was at least a picture of it.

* * *

LET us contrast the picture drawn by Liszt with the one drawn by George Sand.

In it Chopin appears as a curiously secretive and self-centred creature. "He sought for nothing and would have disdained to ask for anything."[2] If he made but few demands, it was perhaps because he was secretly extremely exacting, preferring abstention to half-measures; or perhaps it was due to his sense of his own worth. But one never quite knew what he was thinking, for he never talked of love or friendship. He was generous of everything save himself. He would not give himself. Moreover, he took but little interest in other people's conversations. The serenity of his temper in society was perhaps due to his indifference. When the Utopias of George Sand's democratic friends became too irritating to his subtle intelligence, he would pace silently to and fro at the end of the room, with an expression of slight impatience on his face. He would not start a discussion upon any subject which he had at heart. He was a sincere Catholic, but one might be in his society for a long time without getting to know his religious ideas. Nor did he talk much about Poland. He politely evaded encroaching friendships. But his reserve was not in the least sullen; he would withdraw into himself under cover of a pleasant manner. No doubt he had some whims, some unexpected oddities, a few faults excusable in a sensitive and suffering artist. But most usually he was gay, full of jests, protecting himself when necessary by adroit sarcasms. He was easily wounded, but did not bear any grudge. By his very charm he was able to escape from indiscreet intrusions. Liszt sometimes saw him turn pale with emotion; but in the midst of this emotion he would remain self-controlled, and even his first words were composed. Though his spirit was vehement, this violence was not apparent, whether it was that he repressed it by an effort of will, or that his physical weakness forbade him to give way to it. He endured "the feminine martyrdom of tortures that could never be confessed." His music was his sole confidant. In his works he poured out all his emotions, his sadness, and his suppressed prayers. But even in his art, he desired a certain reserve. Uncultivated roughness repelled him. Everything resembling melodrama, whether in music or literature, was a torture to him.

He did not wish everything to be said. An art which left nothing to the imagination would have seemed to him immodest. He loved what was divined and half-perceived. There was something celestial about his genius. Forests and deserts were repugnant to him. He needed the blue heavens.

* * *

THE *Histoire de ma vie* is very reticent about the breach. George Sand recognises that she did not share either Chopin's tastes, his ideas — outside of art — his political principles, or his way of looking at facts, which means that Chopin was a Catholic and not a democrat, loved society and was uncompromising in his judgments. These were the delicate points, unequal in their importance, but a clash over which might serve as a pretext for a quarrel. It is certain that Chopin's Catholicism seemed to George Sand a childish and deplorable superstition: "The death of his friend, Dr. Matuszyński, and, close after it, that of his own father, dealt him two terrible blows. Catholic dogma clothes death with hideous terrors. Instead of dreaming of a better world for these pure souls, Chopin had none but alarming visions, and I was obliged to pass many nights in a room next his, ready to get up from my work a thousand times, and dissipate the visions which haunted him, both waking and sleeping. The thought of his own death appeared to him, surrounded by all the superstitious imaginings of Slav poetry. A true Pole, he lived in the nightmare land of legend. Phantoms beckoned to him and embraced him, and instead of seeing his father and friend smiling at him in the rays of faith, he would push away their emaciated faces from his own, or struggle in the grasp of their icy hands." [3]

But Chopin, for his part, must have been exasperated by George Sand's airs of superiority in approaching these subjects. "He was foreign to my studies, my enquiries, and hence to my convictions," she said of him. Her contempt is palpable, and he must have been rather irritated by it. Another cause of disagreement must have been the uncompromising tone of Chopin's judgments. He could forgive nothing, whereas she forgave many things. "He would never compromise with human nature," she says again. "He would not accept reality. In this lay his vice and his virtue, his greatness and his destitution. Implacable towards the slightest blemish, he had a boundless enthusiasm for the smallest ray of light." [4]

However, just as she assures us that she never tried to

dominate Chopin's personality, she is careful to affirm that Chopin was quite different with her from what he was with others, that for her he was "devotion, consideration, grace, kindness and deference personified." But, racked by illness, he would suddenly seize upon some trivial pretext to hurt the feelings of Maurice, George Sand's son, who had been deeply attached to him up till then. "They would embrace each other a moment afterwards, but the grain of sand had fallen into the peaceful lake, and one by one the pebbles began to fall into it." One day Maurice spoke of leaving the place. George Sand took her son's part. "Chopin could not endure my legitimate and necessary intervention. He hung his head and said that I no longer loved him." She would have us believe that this was the first and last quarrel.

Unfortunately a letter of George Sand's of November 2, 1847, reveals a more painful and dramatic aspect of the truth. "His character became more embittered from day to day," she said; "he had gone so far as to inflict outbursts of vexation, temper and jealousy upon me in the presence of all my friends and of the children. . . . Maurice began to be indignant with him. Knowing and seeing the chastity of my relations, he could also see that this poor suffering spirit involuntarily, and perhaps in spite of himself, posed as a lover, as a husband, as though he had rights over my thoughts and actions. He was on the point of losing his temper, and telling him to his face that he was putting me in a ridiculous position at the age of forty-three, and abusing my kindness, patience and pity for his nervous and suffering condition. A few more months or days of this situation, and perhaps an impossible, a terrible struggle might have broken out between them. . . .

" . . . The poor child was not even able to observe that outward propriety of which he was normally a slave both by principle and habit. Men, women, old people, children, everything became an object of horror and of wild, insensate jealousy; if he had confined himself to showing it to me, I could have borne it, but these outbursts took place before my children, before my servants, before men who, on seeing them, might have lost that respect to which my age and conduct for the last ten years had given me a right, so that I could no longer endure it." [5]

Such are the causes of the rupture as stated by George Sand. Let us not forget that she alone has spoken, and that Chopin was silent.

In the spring of 1847, however, they had still no idea that they were about to leave each other. On April 14 Chopin wrote to his family: " You ask me what I think of doing in the summer: only the same as usual. I shall go to Nohant as soon as it begins to be warm." He mentions Mme. Delphine Potocka's departure for Nice a few days before, and adds: " Before she left, I played my sonata with Franchomme for her at my rooms.[6] The same evening I had also there Prince and Princess Czartoryski and the Princess of Württemberg, as well as Mme. Sand." A week later he finishes his letter: " Yesterday Mme. Sand started with Solange, that cousin whom you know [7] and Luce." Three days go by and he adds: " I have already received a letter from the country." And finally on the 19th: " Yesterday I was interrupted by a letter from Nohant. Mme. Sand wrote to me that she will arrive at the end of next month, and that we must wait for her. Probably the arrangements for Sol (ange)'s marriage are going forward, though no longer with the man of whom I told you.[8] May God grant them all his gifts! If there is anyone worthy of happiness it is indeed Mme. Sand."

George Sand, for her part, writes to Grzymala on May 12, 1847, after Chopin had been ill: " Well, this time he is saved once more, but how dark the future is for me in this respect also! In any case I shall be in Paris for a few days at the end of the month, and if Chopin can be moved, I shall bring him back here." She then breaks into complaints of which we already know the subject. But she adds some fresh details about their intimacy. After saying that for seven years she had lived like a virgin with him and others, she adds: " I am well aware that many people accuse me, some of having exhausted him by the violence of my senses, others of having driven him to despair by my vagaries. I believe you know what the truth really is. As for him, he complains to me that I have killed him by refusing sexual relations, whereas I knew for certain that I should kill him if I acted otherwise. Such is my position in this fatal friendship, in which I have made myself his slave in every way in which I could do so without showing him an impossible and reprehensible preference over my children, and in which the respect which I ought to inspire in my children and friends was such a delicate matter and so important for me to preserve. I have displayed prodigies of patience in this matter, of which I had not believed myself capable. I ended by suffering a perfect martyrdom! But Heaven is inexorable towards me, as though I had great crimes to expiate; for in the midst of all these efforts and sacrifices, he whom I love is dying, a victim to the insensate affection which he continues to feel for me."

* * *

THE marriage of Solange was celebrated on May 20, 1847. Terrible quarrels broke out between the young couple and George Sand. In July the mother writes: " The scenes which forced me, not to show them the door, but to turn them out of it, are incredible and cannot be described. They can be summed up in a few words: the fact is that murder was almost done here; my son-in-law lifted up a hammer to strike Maurice, and would perhaps have killed him if I had not placed myself between them, hitting my son-in-law in the face and receiving a blow in the breast from him. If the priest, who happened to be there, some friends and a servant had not intervened, Maurice, who was armed with a pistol, would have killed him on the spot."
Chopin was in Paris. Solange hurried off to prejudice him in her favour. Chopin let himself be persuaded and ceased to write. George Sand, ill and crazed with anxiety, wanted to go to Paris and discover the cause of this silence: " At last I received by the morning post a letter from Chopin. I saw that, as usual, I had been

the dupe of my stupid heart, and had passed six sleepless nights torturing myself about his health, while he was occupied in speaking and thinking ill of me with the Clesingers. Very good! His letter is absurd in its dignity, and the sermons of this excellent father of a family will indeed serve me as a lesson. Once warned, one is on one's guard, and in future I shall be quite calm about this matter." She answered Chopin in a letter which " one must admit to be cruel," as Delacroix, to whom Chopin read it, wrote on July 20.

This happened in July. On August 14, George Sand writes: " As for Chopin, I never hear a word about him, and I beg you to tell me how he really is: no more. The rest does not interest me at all, and I have no cause to regret his affection."

Chopin, on the contrary, was inconsolable. We cannot reject Liszt's testimony: " In spite of the arts employed by his friends to keep this subject out of his memory, in order to prevent the dangerous emotion which it caused, he loved to revert to it, as if he wished to stupefy himself with this fatal balm." [9] And later: " Chopin felt and often repeated that in breaking this long affection, this powerful bond, he had broken his life." [10]

THESE tragic years of 1846 and 1847 saw the appearance of Chopin's last works. In January 1846 he published three Mazurkas (op. 59); in September the Barcarolle (op. 60), the Polonaise fantaisie (op. 61) and two Nocturnes (op. 62).

The Barcarolle is definitely in lied form in 12/8 time, with that wave-like accompaniment which Schumann and Mendelssohn had used in their gondoliers' songs. This is why Niecks is able to write that there is no lack of local colour in it, and Tausig to hold that it represented a love-scene in a discreet gondola. But Chopin's picturesque titles — bolero, tarantella, barcarolle — are rather indications of rhythm than pictorial evocations. In fact, the Barcarolle is a nocturne in two parts, harmonised sometimes in sixths, sometimes in thirds. The opening theme is a period of which the first figure, in F sharp minor, is as follows:

This figure, repeated a fourth higher, forms the first phrase of the period; the second phrase, in accordance with a frequent practice of Chopin, being based on a fresh motive. The development is carried out in other periods, of a full and charming character. The piece is one continuous cantilena. By a modulation in A major we arrive at the second group, or central group of the lied, the theme of which is as follows:

A modulation in C sharp major, at which point Chopin indicates a *dolce sfogato,* represents, if Tausig is to be believed, a kiss. After which there is a return to the opening theme, restated in its original key of F sharp major.

Maurice Ravel has given a graceful description of the charm of the Barcarolle. " The theme in thirds is simple and delicate, and constantly adorned with dazzling harmonies. The melodic line is unbroken. A chant-like melody detaches itself, hangs momentarily suspended, and droops softly downwards, attracted by the magical chords. The emotion grows more intense. A new and magnificently lyrical theme is sounded, having quite an Italian character. A calm falls. A rapid, quivering run rises from the depths, and floats above the rare and tender harmonies. One is reminded of some mysterious apotheosis."

The year 1847 saw the appearance in September of three Mazurkas (op. 63) and three Waltzes (op. 64).

We may remember that the Sonata for piano and violoncello (op. 65), which appeared in October, had been composed two years before. It closes the list of works which appeared during Chopin's lifetime. It may be said that after the breach with George Sand he never composed again.

CHAPTER 2

As early as 1839 Chopin had been very ill. "Alas, he suffered greatly," writes Mme. Streicher, who was his pupil at the time. "Weak, pale and coughing, he often took drops of opium with sugar and gamboge water, and bathed his brow with eau de Cologne; in spite of all, he taught with wonderful patience, perseverance and zeal." From that time onwards his health grew worse and worse. Eight years later, at the time of the breach with George Sand, he was no more than a shadow. "From 1846 to 1847 he hardly walked any more, being unable to go upstairs without a painful sensation of stifling; after that time he only kept alive by dint of care and precautions." [1] He only went out in a carriage. When he had business at Schlesinger's, he did not leave his carriage; one of the assistants came out to him, and he stayed there wrapped up in his blue cloak.[2]

In the spring of 1847 he had an illness from which he was not expected to recover. Yet he was able to give a concert on February 16, 1848. The tickets were 25 francs each, an enormous price at that time, and could not be obtained without influence. "Besides the aristocracy of elegant women, there were present," says the *Gazette musicale* of February 20, " the aristocracy of artists and amateurs, happy to catch this sylph of music on the wing. . . . The sylph kept his word, and with what success, what enthusiasm! It is easier to tell you of the welcome he received, and the ecstasies he aroused, than to describe, analyse and reveal the mysteries of an execution which has not its like in our earthly sphere. Even if we had at our command the pen which traced the delicate wonders of Queen Mab . . . it would be all we could do to manage to give you an idea of a purely ideal talent, into which matter hardly enters at all."

Chopin had as a pupil Jane Wilhelmina Stirling, a rich, clever Scotswoman living in Paris, to whom he dedicated in 1844 the two Nocturnes of op. 55. She pressed him to go to London. He was not very anxious to stay in Paris after the revolution of February, 1848, and resolved to make the journey to England. He arrived in London on April 21, took a fine lodging for £80 in Dover Street, and gave two concerts, one at Lord Falmouth's house, the other at that of Mrs. Sartoris, which brought him nearly 300 guineas; he also played at three evening parties, at one of which, at the Duchess of Sutherland's house, he played before the

Queen. He was paid twenty pounds for each of these evening parties.

From London he went on to Edinburgh, and from there he was taken to Calder House, the residence of Lord Torphichen, Jane Stirling's brother-in-law; then to Keir, the abode of the Stirling family, and to Johnston Castle. On August 28 he played at Manchester, on September 27 at Glasgow, on October 4 at Edinburgh. On October 1 he wrote from Keir to Grzymała: "I am getting worse every day. I feel progressively weaker; I am incapable of composing, not because I do not want to, but for purely physical reasons, and because I move from one place to another every week." At the beginning of November he was back in London, and in January, 1849 he returned to Paris. Delacroix, who saw him on January 29, writes: "As for Chopin, his sufferings prevent him from taking an interest in anything, most of all in his work." [3]

He burned the manuscripts which he had started, leaving nothing finished but one last nocturne and a very short valse.[4] He even ceased giving lessons.[5]

Nevertheless his fits of depression alternated with those moments of confidence which sufferers from his malady never lose right up to the end. At the beginning of the summer he left the Square d'Orléans for a lodging in the Rue de Chaillot,[6] on the second floor, with a fine view over Paris. Pious friends led him to believe that the apartment cost 200 francs. It cost double that; and the Countess Obrzeskow paid the difference.

It was from the Rue de Chaillot that he wrote on June 25 asking the Jendrzejewicz family to undertake the journey to Paris. He wrote in magnificent weather, in the drawing-room from which he could admire " the panorama of the whole of Paris: its towers, the Tuileries, the Chambers, Saint Germain l'Auxerrois, Saint Etienne du Mont, Notre Dame, the Panthéon, Saint-Sulpice, the Val de Grâce, the five windows of the Invalides, and between these buildings and me, nothing but gardens." The letter is urgent, but not depressed. Whether deliberately, or under the influence of his illusions, Chopin affects to be hopeful. But who knows what anguish is concealed in his anxiety to see his friends? " My dearly loved ones, come if you can. I am ill and no doctor can help me as you can. If money is wanted, borrow it; when I am better I shall easily earn some, and will repay it to the person who lends it to you.[7] I do not know myself why I am so anxious to see Louise; it is like the longing of a pregnant woman. I vow to you that it will be a good thing for her too. I hope the family council will send her to me: who knows whether I may not bring her back when I am well! How happy we shall all be then, and how we shall clasp one another in our arms."

Mme. Jendrzejewicz hastened to the spot. Chopin lingered on for the whole of the summer. " His weakness and his sufferings had become so great," says Berlioz, " that he could no longer let anyone hear him play the piano, or even compose; even the slightest conversation made him alarmingly tired. He tried in general to make himself understood as much as possible by signs." [8]

The lodging in the Rue de Chaillot was a summer residence. His friends Albrecht and O'Meara found him a final lodging at 12, Place Vendôme. He moved in at the end of September. From the begining of October he could no longer stand up without being supported. His sister and his pupil Gutmann did not leave him for a minute. He held Gutmann's hand almost uninterruptedly. The Abbe Jelowicki gave him the viaticum on the 13th. On the 15th the sick man's voice failed him. On that day the beautiful Countess Delphine Potocka, who had hastily returned, came to see him. He asked her to sing. The piano from the sitting-room was rolled up to his bedroom door. The Countess choked down her sobs and sang. She was interrupted in the middle of the second song by his death-rattle. The piano was pushed back, and nobody was left by his bedside save the priest reciting the prayers for the dying, and his kneeling friends.[9]

This was the end. The night was terrible. On the morning of October 16 he became a little better. Twice during the day Chopin summoned to his bedside the friends gathered in the sitting-room. He had a word for each of them. He recommended the faithful Franchomme to Princess Czartoryska. " You will play Mozart together," he said, " and I shall hear you." On that same day he received the last sacraments. He was resting on Gutmann's shoulder. He had his eyes closed, and his laboured breathing was audible. At the end of the prayers he opened his eyes and said Amen. During the evening, Dr. Cruveille asked him whether he was suffering. The dying man was distinctly heard to say " *Plus.*" Between three and four in the morning, Gutmann gave him something to drink. Chopin murmured " *Cher ami* " and died. Gutmann kept the glass with the imprint of his lips upon it.

His face had become radiant in its beauty. Clesinger took a cast of it, and Kwiatkowski made a drawing. The funeral took place at the Madeleine on October 30. Once more his works fell upon his now unhearing ears.

The Funeral March, orchestrated by Reber, was performed at the Introit. At the Offertory, Lefébure-Wély played the Preludes in B minor and E minor on the organ. Chopin had himself desired that Mozart's Requiem should be performed. Lablache sang the *Tuba Mirum:* he had sung it in 1827 at Beethoven's funeral. Meyerbeer and Prince Adam Czartoryski led the funeral procession. Prince Alexander Czartoryski, Delacroix, Franchomme and Gutmann were the pall-bearers.

* * *

IN writing this brief biography, I have consulted the historians and Chopin's works. But whatever pains one may take, an analysis of this sort misses the essential thing. Each musician constructs himself an invisible universe out of the sounds which he links together. We have tried to sketch its plan. But Chopin cannot be imprisoned even in this aerial palace. He lives in fairyland. Liszt relates how he met Heine there, and how they exchanged news of the land where the laughing nymphs have green tresses and veils of silver. There the roses blaze with a noble flame and the trees murmur in the moonlight. The music of Chopin is created out of these flames and these murmurs.

NOTES TO PART FOUR

[1] M. Karenine relates an amusing story about the portrait of Karol, which Chopin's friends copied as if it was his. It was painted by a "lady of the great world" from whom M. F. Hoesick in the first volume of his Chopin borrowed it as representing the musician, whereas it only represents Karol.

[2] F. Liszt, *op. cit.*, p. 175.

[3] George Sand, *Histoire de ma vie*, IV, p. 470.

[4] George Sand, *op. cit.*, IV, p. 467.

[5] W. Karenine, George Sand, III, pp. 529–530. These outbreaks of jealousy, which are carefully hidden in *L'histoire de ma vie*, appear in *Lucrezia Floriani.* In that work Karol is jealous of the parish priest, of a beggar, a servant, a pedlar, a great oaf of a cousin. Liszt is very hard on George Sand, it is true, and gives us to understand that Chopin would no longer tolerate constancy without fidelity. "A moment came when this factitious existence, which could no longer succeed in galvanising the fibres which had wasted away under the eyes of the artist's spiritual beliefs, seemed to him to have gone beyond what his honour could allow him to close his eyes to." *Op. cit.*, p. 285.

[6] The Sonata for piano and violoncello, op. 65.

[7] Augustine Brault.

[8] Solange was to have married a neighbour in the country, but fell in love with Clesinger the sculptor and broke off her first engagement. Chopin was hostile to Clesinger, and with reason. But, as always, George Sand accused him of not seeing things fairly and not understanding human nature. She asked Grzymala to give him to understand that he must not interfere in this affair.

[9] Franz Liszt, *op. cit.*, p. 286.

[10] *Ibid.*, p. 288.

[1] F. Liszt, *op. cit.*, p. 281.

[2] F. Niecks, *op. cit.*, II, p. 309. Niecks was told this by Edward Wolff.

[3] Shortly after his return to Paris, he lost his old doctor, Dr. Molin. "After this he kept changing, dissatisfied with everybody, and trusting the skill of none." F. Liszt, *op. cit.*, p. 294.

[4] F. Liszt, *op. cit.*, pp. 294–295.

[5] He would have been in great straits if Miss Stirling had not heard of it and sent him 25,000 francs. The sum was a long time reaching him, for the concierge kept the envelope. Chopin accepted only part of what was sent him. There are different versions of this story, recorded by Niecks, II, p. 312 sq.

[6] And not at the end of August, as Niecks writes (II, p. 311). Niecks was misled by the fact that Chopin kept his lodging in the Square d'Orléans. In the letter of June 25 he proposes to lodge his brother-in-law Jendrzejewicz in it. On August 20 he dates a letter from there to Titus Woyciechowski. It is possible that he went there between his stay in the Rue de Chaillot and his move to the Place Vendôme.

[7] M. Karlowicz, *op. cit.*, p. 50.

[8] *Journal des Débats,* October 27, 1849.

[9] The account of Chopin's dying moments was written by M. Gavard, who witnessed them. His manuscript was used by Karasowski and by Niecks. Gavard's sister was a pupil of Chopin's, and he dedicated the Berceuse to her.

APPENDIX

CHOPIN'S WORKS.

1825.	Op. 1.	First Rondo for piano. *Dedicated to Madame von Linde.*
1830.	Op. 2.	*La ci darem la mano,* with variations for piano and an accompaniment for orchestra. *Dedicated to M. Woyciechowski.*
1833.	Op. 3.	Introduction and Polonaise brillante, for piano and violoncello. *Dedicated to M. Joseph Merk.*
1851.	Op. 4.	Sonata for piano. *Dedicated to M. Joseph Elsner. (Published posthumously.)*
1827.	Op. 5.	Rondo in the style of a mazurka for piano. *Dedicated to Countess Alexandrine de Moriolles.*
1832.	Op. 6.	Four Mazurkas for piano. *Dedicated to the Countess Pauline Plater.*
——	Op. 7.	Five Mazurkas for piano. *Dedicated to Mr. Johns.*
1833.	Op. 8.	First Trio for piano, violin and violoncello. *Dedicated to Prince Anthony Radziwill.*
——	Op. 9.	Three Nocturnes for piano. *Dedicated to Mme. Camille Pleyel.*
——	Op. 10.	Twelve Grand Etudes for piano. *Dedicated to Mme. Camille Pleyel.*

1833.	Op. 11.	Grand Concerto for piano with orchestra. *Dedicated to M. Kalkbrenner.*
——	Op. 12.	Variations brillantes for piano on the favourite Rondo from Herold's *Ludovic:* "Je vends des scapulaires." *Dedicated to Miss Emma Horsford.*
1834.	Op. 13.	Grand Fantasia on Polish airs, for piano with orchestra. *Dedicated to M. J. P. Pixis.*
——	Op. 14.	Krakowiak, Grand Concert Rondo for piano, with orchestra. *Dedicated to the Princess Adam Czartoryska.*
——	Op. 15.	Three Nocturnes for piano. *Dedicated to M. Ferd. Hiller.*
——	Op. 16.	Rondo for piano. *Dedicated to Mlle. Caroline Hartmann.*
——	Op. 17.	Four Mazurkas for piano. *Dedicated to Mme. Lina Freppa.*
——	Op. 18	Grand Valse for piano. *Dedicated to Miss Laura Horsford.*
——	Op. 19.	Bolero for piano. *Dedicated to the Countess E. de Flahault.*
——	Op. 20.	First Scherzo for piano. *Dedicated to M. T. Albrecht.*
1836.	Op. 21.	Second Concerto for piano with orchestra. *Dedicated to the Countess Delphine Potocka.*
——	Op. 22.	Grand Polonaise brillante preceded by an Andante spianato. *Dedicated to the Baroness d'Est.*

1836. Op. 23. Ballade for piano. *Dedicated to the Baron Stockhausen.*

1835. Op. 24. Four Mazurkas. *Dedicated to the Comte de Perthuis.*

1837. Op. 25. Twelve Etudes for piano. *Dedicated to the Comtesse d'Agoult.*

1836. Op. 26. Two Polonaises for piano. *Dedicated to M. J. Dessauer.*

—— Op. 27. Two Nocturnes for piano. *Dedicated to the Countess Apponyi.*

1839. Op. 28. Twenty-four Preludes for piano. *Dedicated to his friend Pleyel.* (*The German edition is dedicated to J. C. Kessler.*)

1838. Op. 29. Impromptu for piano. *Dedicated to the Countess Lobau.*

—— Op. 30. Four Mazurkas for piano. *Dedicated to the Princess of Württemberg, née Princess Czartoryska.*

—— Op. 31. Second Scherzo for piano. *Dedicated to the Countess Adèle von Fürstenstein.*

1837. Op. 32. Two Nocturnes for piano. *Dedicated to the Baroness Billing.*

1838. Op. 33. Four Mazurkas for piano. *Dedicated to the Countess Mostowska.*

—— Op. 34. Three Valses Brillantes for piano. *Dedicated No 1 to Mlle. de Thun-Hohenstein; No 2 to Mme. G. d'Ivri; No 3 to Mlle. A. d'Eschtal.*

1840. Op. 35. Sonata for piano.

—— Op. 36. Second Impromptu for piano.

1840.	Op. 37.	Two Nocturnes for piano.
——	Op. 38.	Second Ballade for piano. *Dedicated to M. R. Schumann.*
——	Op. 39.	Third Scherzo for piano. *Dedicated to M. A. Gutmann.*
——	Op. 40.	Two Polonaises for piano. *Dedicated to M. J. Fontana.*
——	Op. 41.	Four Mazurkas for piano. *Dedicated to M. E. Witwicki.*
——	Op. 42.	Valse for piano.
——	Op. 43.	Tarantella for piano.
——	Op. 44.	Polonaise for piano. *Dedicated to the Princess Charles de Beauvau.*
——	Op. 45.	Prelude for piano. *Dedicated to the Princess Elizabeth Czernicheff.*
——	Op. 46.	Allegro de concert for piano. *Dedicated to Mlle. F. Müller.*
——	Op. 47.	Third Ballade for piano. *Dedicated to Mlle. P. de Noailles.*
——	Op. 48.	Two Nocturnes for piano. *Dedicated to Mlle. L. Duperré.*
——	Op. 49.	Fantaisie for piano. *Dedicated to the Princess C. de Souzzo.*
——	Op. 50.	Three Mazurkas for piano. *Dedicated to M. Léon Szmitkowski.*
1843.	Op. 51.	Allegro Vivace. Third Impromptu for piano. *Dedicated to the Countess Eszterházy.*
——	Op. 52.	Fourth Ballade for piano. *Dedicated to the Baroness C. de Rothschild.*

1843. Op. 53. Eighth Ballade for piano. *Dedicated to M. A. Leo.*

—— Op. 54. Scherzo No. 4 for piano. *Dedicated to Mlle. J. de Caraman.*

1844. Op. 55. Two Nocturnes for piano. *Dedicated to Miss J. W. Stirling.*

—— Op. 56. Three Mazurkas for piano. *Dedicated to Miss C. Maberly.*

1845. Op. 57. Berceuse for piano. *Dedicated to Mlle. Élise Gavard.*

—— Op. 58. Sonata for piano. *Dedicated to the Comtesse E. de Perthuis.*

1846. Op. 59 Three Mazurkas for piano.

—— Op. 60. Barcarolle for piano. *Dedicated to the Baroness Stockhausen.*

—— Op. 61. Polonaise-fantaisie for piano. *Dedicated to Mme. A. Veyret.*

—— Op. 62. Two Nocturnes for piano. *Dedicated to Mlle. R. de Konneretz.*

1847. Op. 63. Three Mazurkas for piano. *Dedicated to the Countess Czosnowska.*

—— Op. 64. Three Valses for piano. *Dedicated No 1 to the Countess Potocka; No 2 to the Baroness Rothschild; No 3 to the Baroness Bronicka.*

—— Op. 65. Sonata for piano and violoncello. *Dedicated to M. A. Franchomme.*

* * *

In 1855, Fontana published a collection of posthumous works, which he numbered 66 to 74. They include: Op. 66,

Fantaisie-impromptu; Op. 67, Four Mazurkas; Op. 68, Four Mazurkas; Op. 69, Two Valses; Op. 70, Three Valses; Op. 71, Three Polonaises; Op. 72, Nocturne, Funeral March and Three Ecossaises; Op. 73, Rondo for two pianos; Op. 74, Seventeen Polish Melodies.

During Chopin's lifetime, a certain number of pieces appeared without an opus number. They include: in 1833 the *Grand duo concertant* for piano and violoncello on themes from *Robert the Devil,* by F. Chopin and A. Franchomme; in 1840, Three Etudes in the *Méthode des Méthodes* of Moscheles and Fétis; in 1842, a Mazurka in A minor in an album published by Schott and entitled *Notre Temps.*

Finally, a certain number of posthumous works have been published outside of Fontana's collection. In 1851 Haslinger brought out at the same time as the Sonata Op. 4 some Variations for the piano on a German air, of which he had had the manuscript since 1830. Niecks mentions (II, pp. 358–359) a dozen Mazurkas, Valses and Polonaises of next to no value which appeared at various dates. A 26th Prelude was published at Geneva in 1918. Cp. Ed. Ganche, *op. cit.* pp. 93–99.

BIBLIOGRAPHY

G. Jean Aubry. *Hommage à Chopin*, Paris, 1916.

Mme. A. Audley. *Frédéric Chopin, sa vie et ses œuvres*, Paris, 1880 (Plon).

H. Barbedette. *F. Chopin, Essai de critique musicale.* Paris, 1869 (Heugel).

Henry T. Finck. *Chopin and other Musical Essays.* New York, 1899 (Scribner).

Édouard Ganche. *Frédéric Chopin, sa vie et ses œuvres*, Paris, 1908 (Mercure de France). 5th Edition, revised 1921.

——, *Dans le souvenir de Frédéric Chopin*, Paris, 1925 (Mercure de France).

J. Cuthbert Hadden. *Chopin.* London, 1903 (Dent).

Ferdynand Hoesick. *Chopin, Życie i tworczość* (His life and productions) t. I 1810–1831. Warsaw, 1904 (preface dated from Saint Enogat, 1902).

——, *do. do.*, 3 vols. t. I (1810–1831); t. II (1831–1845); t. III (1845–1849). Warsaw and Cracow, 1911 (preface partly similar to that of 1902, dated from Cracow, 1911).

James Huneker. *Chopin, the man and his music*, 1900. German translation *Chopin der Mensch, der Künstler*, by Lola Lorme, Munich (Georg Müller), 2nd ed. 1920, 3rd and 4th ed. 1921.

M. Karasowski. *Młodość Chopina* (Chopin's Youth), Warsaw, 1862; 2nd ed. 1869.

——, *Friedrich Chopin, Sein Leben, seine Werke und Briefe,* (Life, Works and Letters), 2 vols. Dresden (von Ries), 1877. There were three editions during the author's life, 1877, 1878 and 1881. There is a one volume edition, without date, *Friedrich Chopin, sein Leben und seine Briefe, neue Ausgabe* (von Ries and Esler). In this edition the two last chapters of the original edition, *Chopin als Mensch* and *Chopin als Componist* are omitted. There is a Polish edition (1882): *Fryderyk Chopin, Życie, Listy, Dzieła.*

Mieczysław Karlowicz. *Souvenirs inédits de Fréderic Chopin,* translated by Laura Disière, Paris and Leipzig, 1904 (Welter). The Polish edition (Vol. I of the Publications of the Warsaw Musical Society, section *Chopin,* contains a dozen letters from George Sand to Mme. Jendrzejewicz and five from Solange Clésinger to Chopin, which do not appear in the French edition.

Jean Kleczyński. *Fréderic Chopin. De l'interprétation de ses œuvres.* Three lectures delivered in Warsaw. Paris, 1880 (Noel).

——, *Chopin's grössere Werke,* Leipzig, 1898 (Breitkopf).

F. Liszt. *F. Chopin.* Leipzig, 1852. (Breitkopf and Härtel). 2nd ed. 1879; 6th ed. 1923. The work is dated Weimar 1850; it first appeared in *La France Musicale,* 1851.

Frédérick Niecks. *Frederick Chopin as a man and musician,* 2 vols. London, 1888. 3rd ed. 1903 (Novello).

Henryk Opieński. *Chopin.* Levous, 1910 (Altenberg).

Élie Poirée. *Chopin.* Paris, 1907 (Laurens).

Bernard Scharlitt. *Friedrich Chopins Gesammelte Briefe.* Leipzig, 1911 (Breitkopf).

Josef Sikorski. *Wspomnienie Szopena* in the *Bibliothèque de Varsovie,* 1849, t. 36, pp. 510–559.

A. Sowiński. *Słownik muzyków polskich,* Paris, 1874.

Henryk Strenger. *O życiu Chopina, gienjuszu i duchu jego muzyki* (On Chopin's life and genius and the spirit of his music), Warsaw, 1910 (Wende).

M. A. Szulc. *Fryderyk Chopin i utwory jego muzyczne* (F. C. and his musical compositions), Posen, 1873 (Zupanski).

Ipolito Valetta. *Chopin. La vita, le opere,* Turin, 1910 (Bocca).

Adolf Weissmann. *Chopin.* Berlin, 1912 (Schuster).

Charles Willeby. *Frédéric–François Chopin.* London, 1892 (Sampson Low).

Count Wodziński. *Les trois romans de Frédéric Chopin,* Paris, 1886 (Calmann-Lévy).

A NOTE ON THE TYPE IN WHICH THIS BOOK IS SET

This book is composed on the Linotype in Bodoni, so-called after its designer, Giambattista Bodoni (1740–1813) a celebrated Italian scholar and printer. Bodoni planned his type especially for use on the more smoothly finished papers that came into vogue late in the eighteenth century and drew his letters with a mechanical regularity that is readily apparent on comparison with the less formal old style. Other characteristics that will be noted are the square serifs without fillet and the marked contrast between the light and heavy strokes.